girl scouts

TAKE ACTION

You Can Make the World a Better Place

Illustrations by Ana Sebastián

HARPER
An Imprint of HarperCollins*Publishers*

HarperCollins Children's Books,
a division of HarperCollins Publishers, 195 Broadway, New York, NY 10007

HarperCollins Publishers,
Macken House, 39/40 Mayor Street Upper, Dublin 1, D01 C9W8, Ireland

Take Action: You Can Make the World a Better Place

harpercollins.com

Library of Congress Control Number: 2025932717
ISBN 978-0-06-331779-6

Typography by Stephanie Hays
25 26 27 28 29 PC/CWR 10 9 8 7 6 5 4 3 2 1

First Edition

CONTENTS

A Note from Girl Scouts 2

Introduction: You Got This! 5

Chapter One: How to Take Action 11

Chapter Two: Where to Take Action 33

Chapter Three: Figure Out the Issue and its Causes 53

Chapter Four: Build Your Team 77

Chapter Five: Pinpoint Your Goal 93

Chapter Six: Check Yourself 119

Chapter Seven: Make Goals and Plans 139

Chapter Eight: Make it Happen 169

Chapter Nine: Celebrate—You Did It! 191

Conclusion: Don't Stop Now 200

A NOTE FROM GIRL SCOUTS

Ever wished there was a skate park in your town or that your neighborhood did a better job recycling? Have you ever felt frustrated that your school library doesn't have your favorite series, or thought the cafeteria food could be way better and healthier? Then this book was written just for you. You don't have to wait until you're a grown-up to make the world a better place! You can do it right now by taking action on the issues you care about—just like generations of Girl Scouts all over the world have done for years. Girl Scouts see opportunities for change and team up with their communities to make it happen. You can be part of this. This is about using your power and helping your school, your neighborhood, and the world. You may not be able to vote, or even drive, but you can make a real impact. Believe in yourself, believe in your strength, and let's do this!

INTRODUCTION: YOU GOT THIS!

Hello, friends!

You probably picked up this book because you want to learn how to make a difference. Well, good news! Just by making that choice, you have *already* used your power. That is huge. You are creating a better world *right now* by being yourself, devoting time to learning, and expressing an interest in helping others.

The secret to creating positive change in the world is knowing how to use your strengths in the best possible way. When you identify your interests, embrace who you are, and decide to lift up your voice, you act as a leader. Girl Scouts around the world have been doing this for over a hundred years, so they're great people to get inspiration from. That's why you'll see stories of Girl Scouts making the world a better place throughout this book. Let their stories and successes motivate you as you discover your passions and learn how to help the world in a fun, collaborative way. If they can do it, so can you!

Consider this book your activist toolbox. As you read, you are going to identify an issue you care about, then embark on a big, exciting journey toward making things better. The stories and exercises in this book will help you identify different types of communities, understand what a bias is, gather a team, and embrace everything else it takes to create positive change. There are six Take Action steps that can help you make the biggest, most lasting impact. And while you don't have to follow them *exactly*, these steps are a great starting point for any meaningful service or leadership project. As Girl Scouts everywhere know, the steps can take the guesswork out of making and then carrying out your exciting (maybe even life changing!) plans.

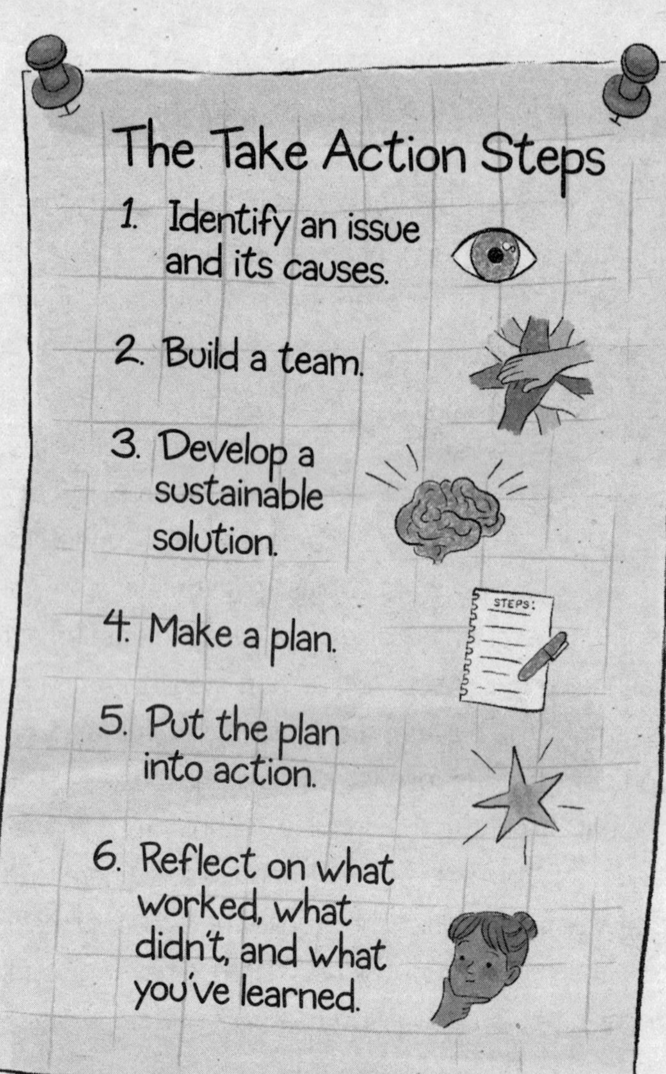

Are you ready?

Amazing! Because *you've got this.*

Take Action Tip

Get a journal or create a DIY one (you can staple pages together or put them together in a folder). Not only is journaling a great way to keep track of your thoughts and ideas, but a lot of the activities in this book involve journaling. Writing down your awesome plans, questions you have along the way, and things you've learned will keep you organized and give you something cool to look back on and feel proud of when you're done!

CHAPTER ONE:

HOW TO TAKE ACTION

Is there a little spark of *something* inside you that lights up when you think about helping others or the world around you? Do you get angry when you see someone at school being bullied, called names, or left out? Ever feel disappointed when you see trash on the playground, and you and your friends just want to have a nice clean place to meet up? If you answered yes to any of these questions—or all three—there's a part of you that wants to step up and help your community do things differently.

The first step, and maybe most important step of making the world a better place, is tapping into your feelings and deciding you want to make a difference in the first place. You don't have to know *exactly* what it is you want to change or how you can go about doing it. You'll get to those things soon. Right now, all you need to know is that if you care and are itching to do *something*, you are ready to step up and get going.

Let's do this!

Journaling: You're Already Making a Difference

Think about the good things you do in the world. Maybe you help your little sister get ready for school in the morning, remind your grandfather to take his medication, or feed the family pet. Those might seem like small tasks, but they make a big difference in the community of your family. Or maybe you've picked up trash at your favorite park or helped at the local food pantry. Grab a journal and write down the amazing things you have done in the past or are already doing. Seeing your accomplishments as a change maker is a terrific way to give you confidence and remind yourself of just how much power you have.

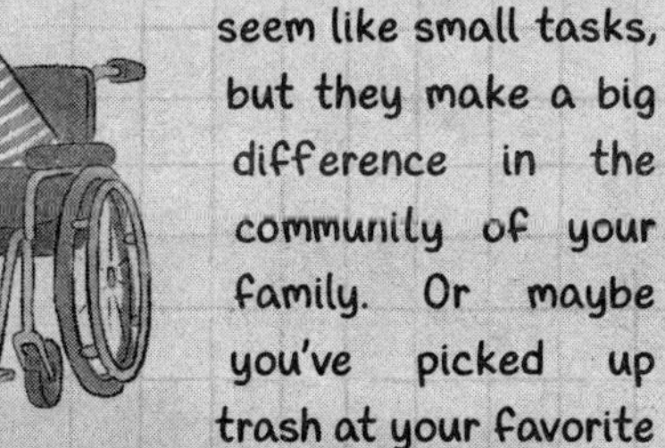

Taking Action and Community Service

What's the difference? Taking action and community service are both incredible ways to make the world a better place, but they aren't exactly the same.

Community service is an act of kindness that adds to efforts that are already in place, and it makes a positive difference *right now*. If you've ever brought cans of food to your school's food drive, donated your old clothes or toys to a neighborhood shelter, or made decorations to brighten a nursing home at the holidays, you've taken part in community service. When lots of people put energy into doing helpful things for others or their communities, it drives big change. Community service is powerful, important, and empowering to volunteers *and* the communities they help. That's why it's sometimes called mutual aid, because the benefits truly affect everyone!

Taking action is a bit more involved than community service. When you take action, you challenge yourself to tackle a big community issue in a deep and long-lasting way. You identify an issue (meaning something you'd like to improve), learn about the root cause of it, then make a plan to change it, not just in the moment, but for a long time—even permanently! When you take action, you work on solving the issue at the *source,* so your impact will last. That's powerful stuff.

For example, let's say you hear that one of your elderly neighbors doesn't want to leave the house during flu season because she is worried about getting sick. So, you consider going grocery shopping for her with your family. That's an awesome act of community service. But what if you realize that you have *lots* of neighbors who don't have a way to easily get groceries? So you decide to start a group that makes weekly grocery trips for anyone who needs them. You may have to find volunteers, create schedules, and spread the word to your neighbors in need—but soon, you'll have a plan and a group of people ready to make a positive, long-term difference. That's what taking action looks like.

Community service and taking action are two ways to help your community, and you can dive into one or the other depending on your schedule, interests, or resources. Here's another way you can think about the difference between them:

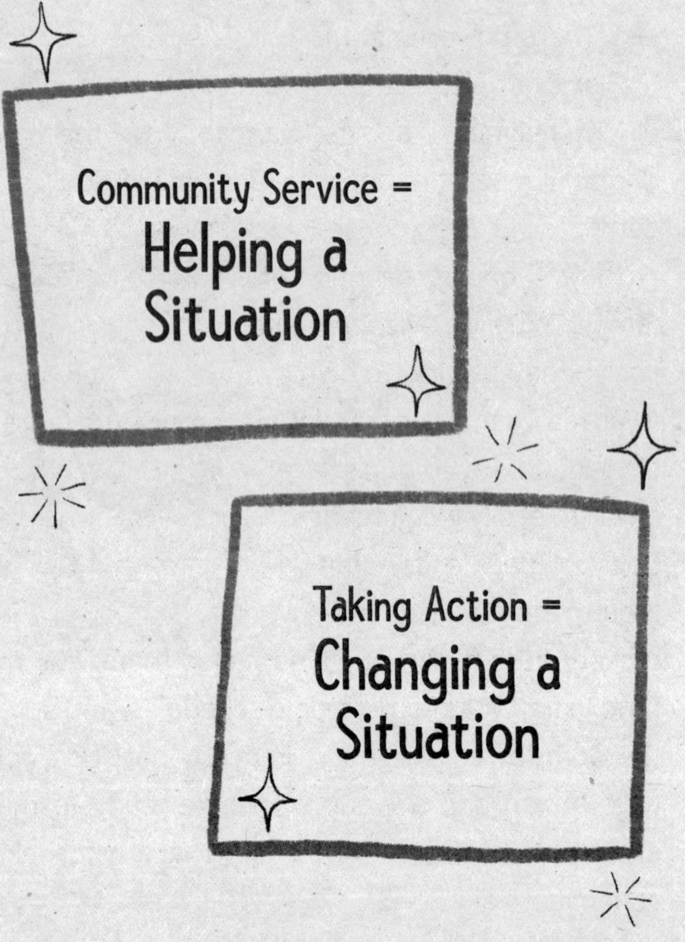

A little confused? That's okay! Here's a chart that might help.

You Care About	You Want to Help (Community Service) So You . . .	You're Ready to Change it (Take Action) So You . . .
Having a clean place to play in your neighborhood	Pick up trash from the playground.	Notice there aren't enough trash cans at the playground, then get your friends, family, and neighbors to ask your local government to buy more through letter writing or speaking at a town council meeting. Keep trying until you get those trash cans!
Helping families who have left home due to domestic violence	Participate in a walk that raises funds and awareness for a local emergency shelter for women and children.	Talk with the shelter staff and discover the families need access to computers so adults can apply for jobs and kids can do homework, then work with the shelter to build a computer lab for them.
Kids who don't have access to the basic resources they need.	Donate your old clothes in the local drop box.	Reach out to families experiencing hardships. Then organize a drop box at your school or local market to collect those specific items and make a plan to distribute them monthly.
Caring for the stray cats in your neighborhood.	Leave food out for the cats in the morning and evening.	Work with a local shelter or animal aid organization to spay or neuter, medically treat, and find forever homes for the cats.

Journaling: What Are Your Community Service or Take Action Ideas?

Hopefully you've already written down how you've already made a difference in the world. Your notes may have sparked new ideas—if so, that's great! If not, don't worry. This book is going to show you exactly how to figure out where you can help.

Below, you'll see a list of issues—these are examples of the types of challenges a community service project or Take Action project might tackle. Read them and then come up with your own ideas of how you'd help each situation right now (through community service) and then for the long-term, through addressing the root of the issue (taking action).

- Issue: It's hard for new kids at my school to meet people and make friends.
- Issue: My local park doesn't have a swing for kids with disabilities.
- Issue: There have been several car crashes at a busy intersection that doesn't have a stoplight.

Now think about some issues you care about. What ideas do you have for community service and/or taking action to address them?

You Can Take Action and Make a Difference

You might be thinking, *But I'm a kid. How can I do something that makes a big, long-lasting impact?* Relax! All you need to do is make one little decision to take part in *anything* that needs your help. Know that almost every positive change starts with one person like you dipping their toes into making a difference.

For example, imagine you start as an occasional volunteer but soon become a central part in changing an organization for the better. While helping out sometimes at a local animal shelter, you fall in love with the animals and can't understand why more families don't come in to adopt them. You soon realize that the shelter doesn't have an up-to-date website that features all the animals' photos. You ask about it, and the head of the shelter tells you they don't have enough money to hire a web designer. So, you approach your school's computer club and ask if they would consider creating an entirely new website for the shelter. They say yes! You take photos of the pets

and give them to the computer club. Within a month, they create a new website. The shelter loves it! After launching it, adoption rates double. It is a win-win for the animals and the people who took home new pets.

One act of community service may inspire you so much that you dream up a big take action idea for a cause you believe in. Or maybe you'll want to get your friends involved to volunteer with you. Whatever you do, just know that you are doing *great* things.

She's Got This!

When she was nine, Claire Sarnowski, a Catholic girl, heard a Jewish Holocaust survivor named Alter Wiener speak about his experience and the family he lost. The two became good friends, and Alter told Claire it was his dream that all students would be required to study the Holocaust so it wouldn't be forgotten. Later when Claire was in middle school and high school, there were several incidents of antisemitism that made Claire even more aware of the need for this type of education. She thought that if people were educated about the Holocaust and other people's histories and cultures, they'd be less likely to hold hateful beliefs or commit acts of hate.

Claire learned that the state legislature decides what gets taught in school, so she called someone at her local school board, who connected her with her state senator. That senator took an interest in her cause and began working with her and Alter to introduce a bill to the Oregon State Legislative Education Committee. Claire and Alter were able to speak in front of this committee, and a few months later the governor signed a bill into law that made Holocaust education part of the curriculum in all Oregon public schools. She even wrote a book about their experiences.

Claire was fourteen—she couldn't drive or vote yet—but she took action and helped create a new law to change what schools teach. Her efforts may even help stop antisemitism at its source. Her friendship with Alter inspired her to learn about her community's needs, build a team, and embark on an amazing journey that made a *huge* difference in her state.

"Anti-Semitism" is discrimination against Jewish people on the basis of religion and/or race.

But how can you figure out what to focus on? How do you tap into an interest that can become a passion project? Maybe you like video games, puppies, tacos, and competition shows—but you wonder what those interests have to do with changing the world. Figuring out what excites you is super important when it comes to taking action. If you feel motivated about something, you're a lot more likely to want to spend time on it. Or if you already spend a lot of energy doing something, it's probably going to be easier for you to spend *more* energy doing that same (or a similar) thing.

Looking inside yourself and thinking about what you care about and what drives you can help you pinpoint where you want to take action. Consider who you are, how you identify, and what (and who) you value. Are there ways you could improve or protect the things that make a difference to those you love? For example, if you or a friend has a disability or a learning difference, maybe the needs of differently abled people are important to you. If you love animals, issues around animal rights and advocacy might be worth diving into.

Siya K. is a Girl Scout from Georgia, and she's a great example of a girl who identified a personal passion and transformed it into a cause. When Siya's grandmother died of oral cancer, Siya was devastated. Not only did Siya love her deeply, but her grandma had helped disadvantaged people in India, and that had been an inspiration to Siya. Siya decided to learn more about oral cancer, and she discovered that it kills one person in the world every hour. In addition, dental disease, which can lead to oral cancer, is one of the most common childhood issues in the world.

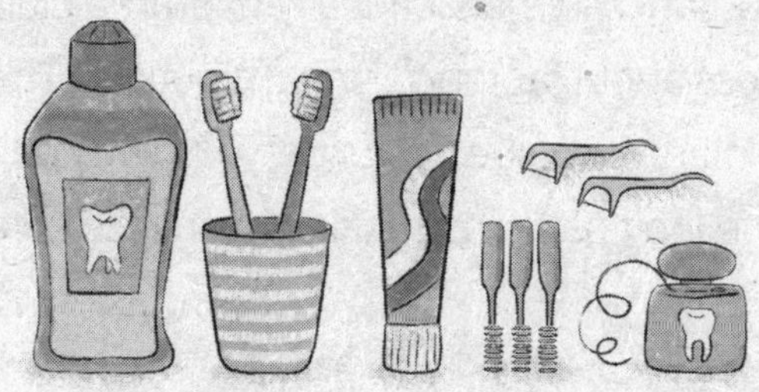

Siya took action and started an organization called "Project Help a Child Smile," which educates people in Georgia and Delhi, India, about taking care of their teeth and gums in order to prevent disease. Siya's love for her grandma led her to take action, and she has now helped thousands of people around the world. She may even be saving lives!

While Siya looked inside her family for inspiration, you can look outside yourself and your surroundings as well. Imagine you live in a city but recently took a school field trip to a nearby farm. There, you saw chickens roaming in a large, fenced yard, eating bugs from the ground and sleeping in roomy coops. When you went home, you decided to read about farming, and you were shocked to learn that many chickens on large industrial farms live in tiny cages, with no opportunity to roam around outside. Just because you don't live on a farm doesn't mean you can't help! You can research and then give your business to companies that treat farm animals ethically or start a club to raise awareness about factory farming practices. Think about communities or issues outside your own bubble; the sky is the limit as far as making change is concerned!

Journaling: What Can You Discover About Your Identity?

Your identity isn't just your name or hair color; it's all the characteristics that come together to make you who you are. No one thing—like being a sports fan, loving art, or coming from a small town—encompasses your full identity. But it's part of it! You are a puzzle of many pieces that match up with each other to make a beautiful whole. Use this journaling activity to think about your identity. It may help you find issues you care about, things that inspire you, and ways to make a difference in the world. You can write, draw, sketch, or express yourself in any way you'd like.

Think about your background: What is your background? Do you have siblings? Do you identify with a particular race, religion, belief system, or nationality? Did your family always live in this country? Do you have a physical, mental, or emotional characteristic that defines part of who you are?

Think about your interests: What do you love to do? Are you a part of any teams? What is your favorite subject in school? What do you like to do in your spare time? Do you have any hobbies or after-school activities that make you really happy?

Think about your home: Do you live with a lot of people or a few? Do you live in a building with a lot of other families or in a building far from others? Have you moved a lot? Do you have access to a backyard or any outdoor space? How has your home impacted you as a person?

Think about your neighborhood: Do you live in a rural, suburban, or urban area? What are your neighbors like? Do you live near any of your family or have neighbor friends? What kinds of businesses are located in your local community? Are there parks where you and your friends feel safe meeting up? Is there anything you wish could be different?

Think about your strengths: What makes you feel proud or powerful? What activity around your house, at school, or community gets you really excited? When you wake up in the morning, what's the first thing on your mind? Is there something you're still working on, but that you've been getting better at over time?

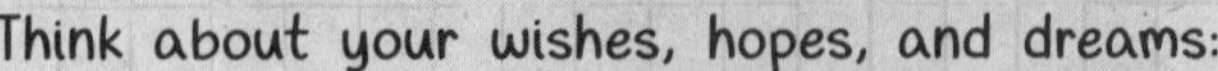

Think about your wishes, hopes, and dreams: What do you wish would be different in your community or even the world? What do you want to be when you grow up? If you could be in charge of your household, your school, or your community for just one day, what would you change and why?

Think about your memories: What is the happiest thing you remember? What was the hardest thing you have ever done or experienced?

Think about your family and friends: What do you love about them? What do you wish you could change? How do you feel when you're around them? What are some of your happiest memories with them?

Taking Action from a Place of Empathy

What drove Claire and Siya to take action is something called "empathy." Empathy is the ability to understand and share the feelings of others. When you are empathetic, you start to imagine the world through someone else's eyes, and you put yourself in their position, attempting to feel their pain and joy as if it were your own.

Maybe it's because they sound so similar, but people often confuse sympathy and empathy. Sympathy is simply feeling bad for someone else. With sympathy, you look at their issues through *your* eyes rather than the other person's. When you have sympathy, you aren't *quite* able to get at the root cause of an issue because you haven't taken the time to learn about the situation or the person who has that issue.

While they are both important, empathy is deep understanding; sympathy is a get-well-soon card. Empathy lasts a lifetime; sympathy lasts a moment.

When you take action, you work from a place of empathy rather than sympathy. Can you tell the difference between the two in the following quiz?

Quiz: Empathy vs. Sympathy

1. When a friend gets a bad grade on a test, you say, "I'm so sorry, maybe you'll do better next time."

A. Sympathy
B. Empathy

2. Your little sister broke her arm and she feels terrible that she can't play soccer with her team for the rest of the season. You know what it's like to miss out on something you wanted to do, so you help her make posters and sit with her at the soccer games to cheer on her team.

A. Sympathy
B. Empathy

3. There's a new student in your school, and no one is very friendly to him. He seems sad. You notice and decide to invite him to your lunch table and ask where he came from, how he's feeling, and if he has any questions or issues. You never want anyone to feel alone.

A. Sympathy
B. Empathy

4. The town next to you is hit by a terrible tornado. People lose their houses and can't go to school or work because they've lost electricity. You and your caregiver decide to drive to the town to clean up fallen trees and help people find temporary places to live. You learn a lot when you talk to these people, and some of their stories make you cry because you remember when your house got flooded and you had to move into a hotel.

A. Sympathy
B. Empathy

5. The boy who lives next door just lost his grandma, so you and your caregiver bake a cake to bring to him and his family.

A. Sympathy
B. Empathy

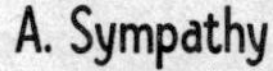

Answers

1. A, 2. B, 3. B, 4. B, 5. A

As you consider raising up that beautiful voice of yours to make change happen, there's one final thing to keep in mind. You may not be old enough to vote or drive yet, and you might be the shyest or smallest person in your class. But you are *never* too young, little, quiet, different (or a million other things) to tap into your passions and make a difference. You are unique, you are the best version of yourself, and you are talented in ways you haven't even discovered yet. You have empathy, and you are passionate about so many things. Your life has so much promise, and you have *years* to figure out what you want to do in this great big life of yours.

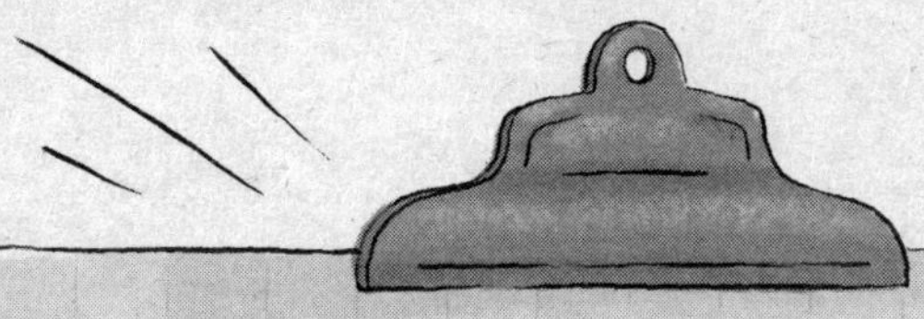

Take Action Tip: Find a Mentor

Claire Sarnowski's mentor was Alter Wiener, the Holocaust survivor she met when she was nine.

Alter was in his late eighties when Claire met him, but your mentor doesn't have to be an adult. You can find mentors at school, in your home, in your extended family, at your Girl Scout troop meetings, in your faith group, through a sports team, or even across the world if you have a pen pal.

They can be almost anyone. That said, mentors should never make you feel unsafe or pressured into anything. In fact, a mentor's job is to support your dreams, encourage your voice, and offer guidance when needed. Look for a mentor you can confide in, ask for advice, and learn from.

CHAPTER TWO:

WHERE TO TAKE ACTION

So you want to change the world?

There are almost eight billion people on planet Earth, and that's a *lot* of folks (of different races, religions, languages, and more!) to try to influence. This doesn't mean you can't do it, though. Look at Melati and Isabel Wijsen. At ten and twelve years old respectively, Isabel and Melati started the Bye Bye Plastic Bag Movement in their city of Bali, Indonesia, an effort to eliminate single-use plastics. Their efforts attracted international media attention, and the sisters went on to speak all over the world to raise awareness about plastic pollution. With the help of their classmates and local community, and six years of work, single-use plastics were officially banned in Bali, and Bye Bye Plastic Bags grew into an international movement with over twenty-five locations around the world!

Isabel and Melati's work has affected thousands (and maybe millions!) of people, but you don't have to reach that far and wide to make a difference. Sometimes changing the life of *one* person in *one* community is the biggest, bravest act of leadership you can undertake. As you start to take action, it's important that you think about the kinds of communities that are all around you—big, small, local, and global—and the many ways you can reach each one. Every community has different needs and ways of doing things, so it's important for changemakers like yourself to think about who you want to help or affect and understand their wants and needs. The more you know about the community you want to reach, the easier it is to take action to help them—and the more powerful it will be when you do!

What Is a Community?

A community is a group of people who share something in common, such as where they live, what they like, what their goals are, what they believe in, or how they identify themselves.

Whether you realize it or not, you're already part of a few communities. These may include your family, your school, your town, your Girl Scout troop, or your sports team. Just know that every member of a community, including you, is equally important, and no one's needs are more important than anyone else's.

Members of a community don't necessarily have *everything* in common. They may not like the same activities, hold similar beliefs, or have the same habits or ways of doing things. For example, the United States is a big community, but there are Americans who love chocolate ice cream and the beach, and there are Americans who prefer sugar cookies and the mountains. Anyone who lives in the United States is part of the community called the United States of America regardless of their likes and dislikes, beliefs, or habits. Still, they may not have much in common at all except that they live in the same country.

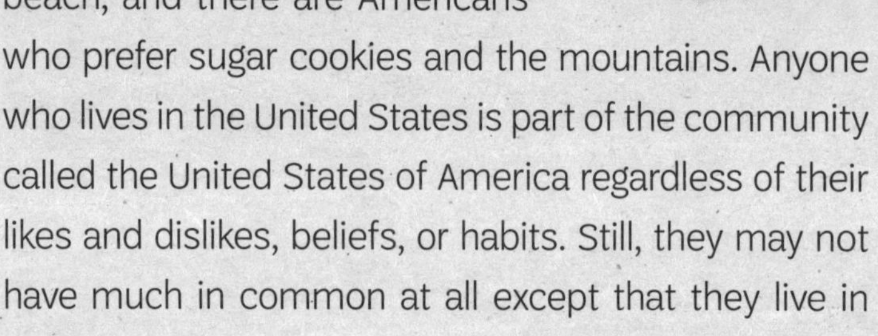

As you explore the different kinds of communities you might help, it's important to remember that differences don't have to mean divisions. We're all in this together!

She's Got This!

Learning to better understand people within your community or in another community is a huge part of making the world a better place. That's exactly what a group of Girl Scouts did.

Many refugees had fled their countries of origin and resettled in the town where these girls lived, yet the girls didn't know much about their new neighbors. They really wanted to understand their experiences—especially what had caused them to leave their homes. Their caregivers also told them that immigration and foreign wars (such as those in Syria and Afghanistan, which had displaced millions of people) were urgent issues in the US, and learning about them was important.

So, the girls decided to create a way to learn about—and even help—refugees. They read books about the lives of refugees throughout history, invited a troop parent to speak about her experience escaping war-torn Vietnam as a child, and spent a day learning about the traditional clothing of some of the local refugee communities. Inspired by what they had learned, they wrote a hundred letters welcoming the new refugee families to their area, worked with two resettlement agencies to gather supplies for them, and created a banner for a troop

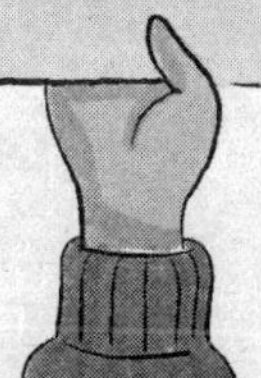

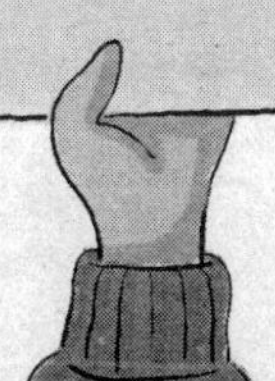

in Jordan made up of refugees from Syria and Iraq (signed "Love from your Girl Scout sisters in the USA").

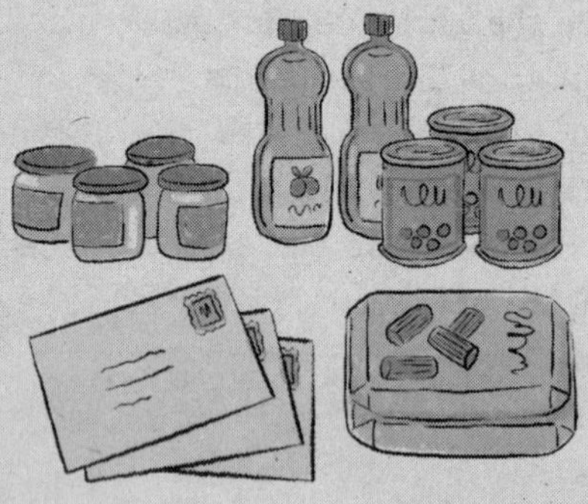

As the girls started to connect with members of the *global* community who had become a part of their *local* community, the refugee experience began to feel personal to them. Soon some of the Girl Scouts shared that their grandparents had been refugees, too, but that they truly didn't understand their histories until they'd imagined walking in their shoes for a day. As one member of the troop said, "I liked helping people understand what a refugee is. Another thing I liked was giving stuff to the group that helps refugees because it helped me imagine what it might feel like to start a new life in a new place."

When you learn about and try to understand others, you can create connections with all different communities.

Types of Communities

There are *so* many different kinds of communities in the world: big ones, small ones, diverse ones, ones built upon similar beliefs, and more! The Girl Scouts in the above "She's Got This" story served both their local community and the global refugee community with their project. As you use your power to help others, you may make a difference in the communities listed below. You may help influence others as well!

Local communities: These are usually bigger than your family and are defined by your geographical area, meaning the city, county, or town you live in. If you live in a city as big as Los Angeles or Chicago, your local community has millions of people! But your local community could also be your school, which may have very few people in it. The common thread in local communities is that there's a shared sense of purpose: you want to keep the community thriving. In your school, people will be happier and do better if it's clean, if there's lots of fun stuff to do at recess, and if the library is well-stocked with great books you can take home. In big cities, the community does best when the parks and biking paths are well-maintained, the air and water are clean, and there are enough homes for everyone to have a safe place to live. In local communities, people rally around taking action and finding solutions to issues including poverty, health care, and even removing snow from sidewalks. Have you ever seen "Shop Local" bumper stickers or signs? Those are to encourage shoppers to think about their community and support the businesses that provide jobs.

Besides towns and schools, other examples of local communities include:

- **Neighborhood associations**
- **Gyms, dojos, or dance studios**
- **Faith groups**
- **Local service organizations, such as the Rotary Club and Woman's Club**
- **Your caregiver's workplace**
- **Girl Scout troops**

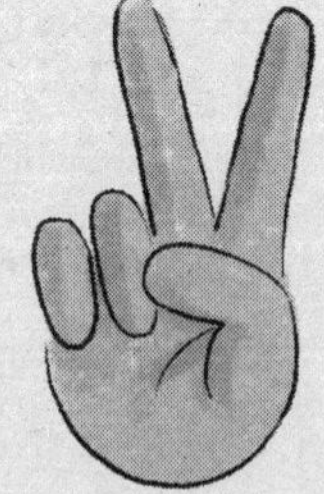

State and national communities: State communities involve your state, and a national community encompasses—you guessed it—your country. Government is one of the major features of state and national communities because elected government officials like the governor, president, senators, representatives, judges, and more make decisions that affect your life. These elected officials decide lots of things, like whether to build a new highway, whether our country should go to war, how to respond to emergencies like earthquakes, and if a beautiful expanse of land should become a park.

State and national communities may also involve *identity*. People who live in California may live near beaches, on farms or mountains, or in big cities, but chances are no matter where they live in the state, they know what their state flag looks like (it has a bear on it!). Americans come in all shapes, sizes, and colors, and live in all kinds of places with a million different beliefs, but all of them identify as *American*. Just like in a local community, most people in state and national communities ultimately hope that their state and country will thrive. They want there to be enough food for everyone and to keep their cities, states, and country safe. They believe in freedom and fairness even if they disagree on what freedom means and what counts as fair.

Besides the government, here are some other examples of state and national communities:

- **State universities**
- **State and national sports leagues**
- **The NAACP, which is the National Association for the Advancement of Colored People. This nonprofit is a**

grassroots organization whose mission is to achieve civil rights and social justice for all.

- Girl Scouts of the USA
- Labor unions, which advocate and fight for the rights of workers

Journaling: How Can You Make a Difference in Your State or Country?

Making a difference on the state or national level isn't something that only politicians (or even just adults!) can do. No matter your age, you can make a difference in the country you call home. Below are some examples how.

- Write your state or national senator or congressperson about a cause you believe in or a change you want made.
- Attend an in person event to support a cause you want to get behind.

- Help adults register to vote.
- Volunteer for a national charity or cause whose mission you support.
- Think about how you can make positive change statewide or nationally—and then write down your ideas. What causes do *you* care about? What do you think you could do to make change across the state or country happen?

Global community: "Global" is something that includes the whole world. The global community is made up of all the people on this planet. Some examples of global communities are:

- **Social media**
- **Online gaming communities**
- **Global fandoms of popstars, book series, and movies**
- **The United Nations, which is an intergovernmental organization that seeks peacekeeping solutions for global issues**
- **Big, international businesses with lots of employees around the world**
- **UNICEF (the United Nations Childrens**

Fund), Amnesty International, and Doctors Without Borders—all international aid organizations

- NATO (the North Atlantic Treaty Organization), an intergovernmental organization including many countries that have vowed to defend each other during war

How to Be a Global Citizen

As you start to think about making the world a better place, it's important to see yourself as a global citizen.

A citizen is someone who belongs to a community of people, so global citizens belong to the global community and think about their role in it. A global citizen who wants to make positive change understands their place in the world and how the decisions they make day-to-day can impact people everywhere. One way or another, all people across the globe are connected, so the choices you make every day affect the eight billion people you share this planet with. Feeling powerful yet? Once you've taken the time to learn about your impact on others around the world, you can think about what choices might help make the planet a better place for everyone.

There are many ways to become an effective global citizen, including the following.

Thinking globally and acting locally: You may have seen this phrase on bumper stickers or billboards. What it means is that even the smallest decisions you make can eventually have a global impact. Did you turn off the lights when you left the bathroom? You helped reduce your carbon footprint, which affects everyone on the planet. If everyone turned off the lights like you did, we could burn fewer fossil fuels, which pollute the atmosphere and contribute to global warming.

Learning about other people and communities: Global citizens are constantly learning about communities and individuals that are different from them. This knowledge helps them better understand other communities' and people's needs. Global citizens try to be empathetic and see the world through others' eyes, and they often study different origins, traditions, beliefs, and more so they can see how their actions affect others.

Becoming open to uncomfortable feelings: Sometimes expanding your worldview can feel a little uncomfortable. Finding yourself in a group of people speaking a language you don't understand, for example, might make you feel left out. Or you might realize something you enjoy or have depended on hurts others. For example, maybe you love shopping at a certain store for clothes, but you learn that the company doesn't pay the people who make the clothes enough money to live on, or that the way they make their clothes hurts the environment. A global citizen may choose to shop elsewhere, even if that means giving up their favorite brand. Finally, as a global citizen, you might have to speak up when it's scary, like when someone of a marginalized race or religion is being treated unfairly at your school. Standing up for others makes you a true citizen of the world.

Being inclusive: Being inclusive means you include everybody—even people who aren't like you or don't believe the same things as you. It also means you make everyone in your group—no matter who they are—feel supported, because they all belong equally. Global citizens understand that, while people have many differences, our differences are actually an opportunity for us learn from each other. Everyone has something to offer. That's why it's important to include people who have differing perspectives and viewpoints when making choices and plans.

The exciting thing is, no matter how you broaden your global mindset, there's always more to learn. There's no finish line! Yes, the world is a big place, but you are a hugely important part of it. You can make a difference, and you *are* making a difference.

A "carbon footprint" is the estimated total amount of pollution produced by an individual, group, or event.

"Marginalized" means that a person or a group has been discriminated against, victimized, or treated like they are insignificant within a community.

Journaling: How to Take Action as a Global Citizen

There are so many ways you can take action in your local, national, or global community. In fact, you may not even know it, but the actions you make every day could be changing the world for the better *right this moment*. If you:

- make an effort to turn off lights when leaving a room or do other things to save energy, you're helping to limit the use of fuel, which is good for the environment.
- do clothing swaps with friends, look for cute outfits at thrift stores, or buy used clothes online, you're helping to reduce waste that could end up in a landfill halfway across the world.

- make and display signs showing support for communities affected by war, violence, or discrimination, you're spreading awareness and showing compassion and kindness to others.

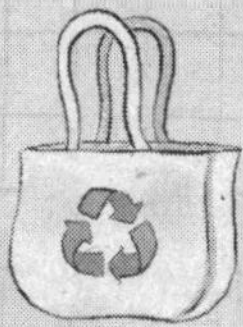

- wash your hands, stay home, or wear a mask when you're not feeling well, you are helping prevent the spread of disease not just in your own community, but globally, since germs can travel from person to person and community to community *fast*.
- stop asking for plastic bags at the grocery store and instead bring your own reusable bags, you're preventing plastic from ending up in the ocean. You tell your friends at school about this, and now they're skipping plastic bags, too. Imagine what will happen if they tell their families and friends!

Take a minute to think about the many ways that you have acted locally and made a global impact because of it. Write them down and think about how much power you have in your day-to-day life. Feels good, doesn't it?

Take Action Tip: Ask So You Can Understand

Don't assume that you understand what a community needs without asking. For example, the Girl Scouts you heard about in Chapter Two reached out to refugee service organizations to ask what refugees need when they come to the US. Then they made a plan to involve their community so everyone could help their new neighbors. People, organizations, or cultures are experts on their own needs. All you have to do is say you'd like to help and want to know the best ways to do that.

CHAPTER THREE:

FIGURE OUT THE ISSUE AND ITS CAUSES

Sometimes it can take time to figure out how you want to help, but don't stress about it. Going slow is a good thing. Rushing into an activity before you've taken time to explore, learn, and dig deep in your heart isn't going to have as meaningful of an impact—for yourself or the people you want to help!

Taking action can take a lot of patience, learning, growth, and time. Sure, it might seem boring to sit around and just *think*, but you need to figure out what you care about before deciding where you want to devote your valuable time and energy (yes, your time has value!). You may feel so ready to take action and make a difference that you want to jump right in—but when you take the time to really, truly think and explore, you are going to achieve even *more* amazing results!

Here's the good news. Just by reading the last two chapters, you've already done a bunch of the prep work that can help you figure out how and where you want to make a difference in the world. You've started to discover what interests you, and you understand what it means to be a global citizen. You have a sense of what drives you and an idea of where your work might be needed. Maybe you've even written some notes, drawn some ideas in your journal, or been inspired by some other amazing young people who are making positive change.

If you're still feeling a little unsure, that's fine, too! Take a deep breath, revisit the activities in those chapters again, talk to someone who believes in you, and brainstorm. There's no rush.

Journaling: Observation Activity

Look around you! Observing and exploring what's happening in your local, national, and global communities is a great way to pinpoint something you're passionate about and want to help change. Don't just think about issues to fix, look at how you can make good things even better! If you want your community to be a happier, more welcoming place, sometimes you just have to ask questions, and you'll notice gaps you can help fill. Use the table below for inspiration as you write observations down in your journal. Then start talking to people, researching, and taking notes on what you've learned. You'll discover ways you can help in no time!

What Do You Notice Around You?	Who Did I Talk to and/or What Research Did I Do?	What Did I Learn?	Maybe I Could . . .
Example: I see a lot of unhoused people asking for food in my neighborhood.	My caregiver and I talked to the head of a local soup kitchen.	The head of the soup kitchen said the lines to get food are so long that some people leave. There just aren't enough volunteers to make the lines move faster. This means some people may go hungry for days at a time.	Develop an online volunteer sign-up form and recruitment campaign for the soup kitchen.
Example: There is a new group of immigrant students in my community, and I've heard some kids saying mean things about their culture.	I talked with a teacher at my school to see if she could help.	She told me a lot of people here have never talked to people from other places in the world and don't understand cultural differences.	Start a school club where we celebrate all backgrounds through learning about cultural diversity.

How to Identify an Issue You Care About

Obviously, you want to dig into an issue that will inspire you *and* produce amazing results. Imagine you love animals and have noticed that there are a lot of stray cats in your neighborhood. You can help! Combine your passion for animals and your community's need to control the stray cat population by forming a Take Action plan that finds them forever homes.

Think about this example of a group of girls just like you. A Girl Scout troop wanted to help their community. To figure out where and how they could assist, they thought about their interests, hobbies, and strengths. They enjoyed a lot of different things like reading, talking to people, and writing, but the one thing they could *all* agree on was how much they loved riding bikes.

Then the girls thought about their community. They lived in the suburbs, so being able to travel on sidewalks was part of what they and their families valued. Unfortunately, in one part of their town, there was a stretch of road with no sidewalk. Not only could they not ride their bikes safely there, but people pushing strollers or driving wheelchairs had to share the street with cars—which can be really dangerous. The girls identified this as a *big issue* and wrote a letter to their town's city manager, asking that the town build a sidewalk. It took a year of advocating, but the city

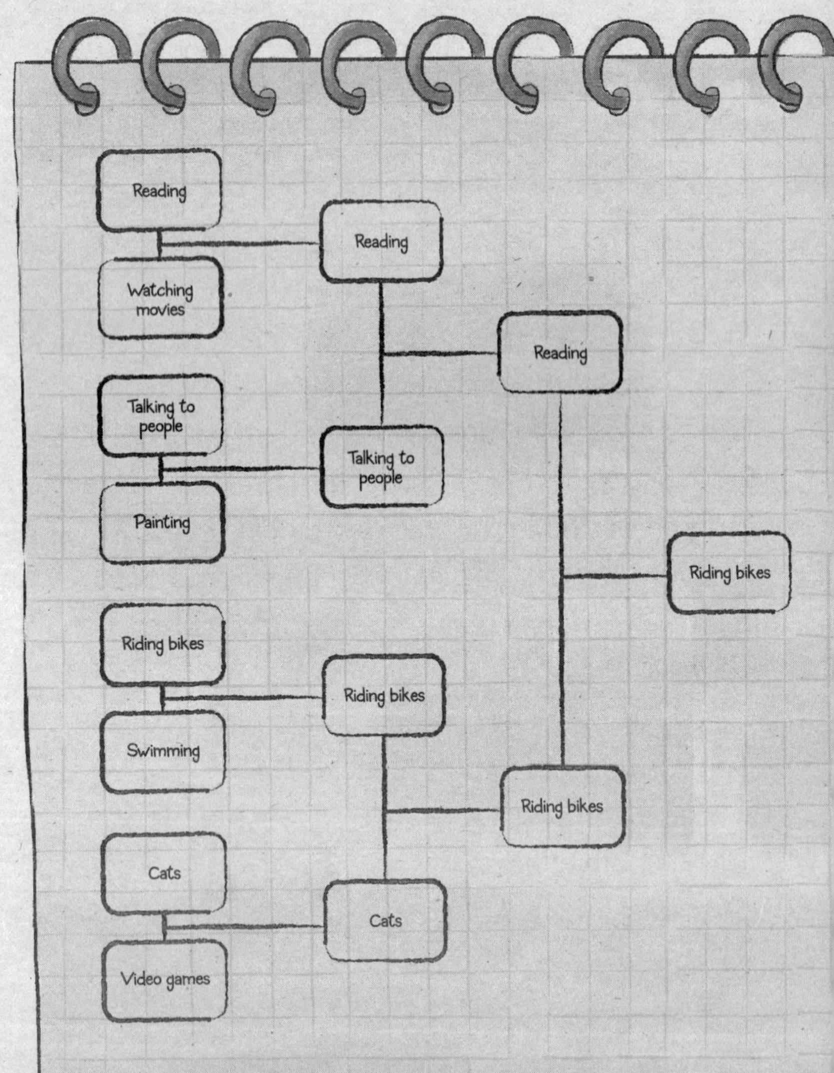

government eventually agreed with them. They built a sidewalk—all thanks to these Girl Scouts speaking up.

You can visualize how to decide where to take action this way:

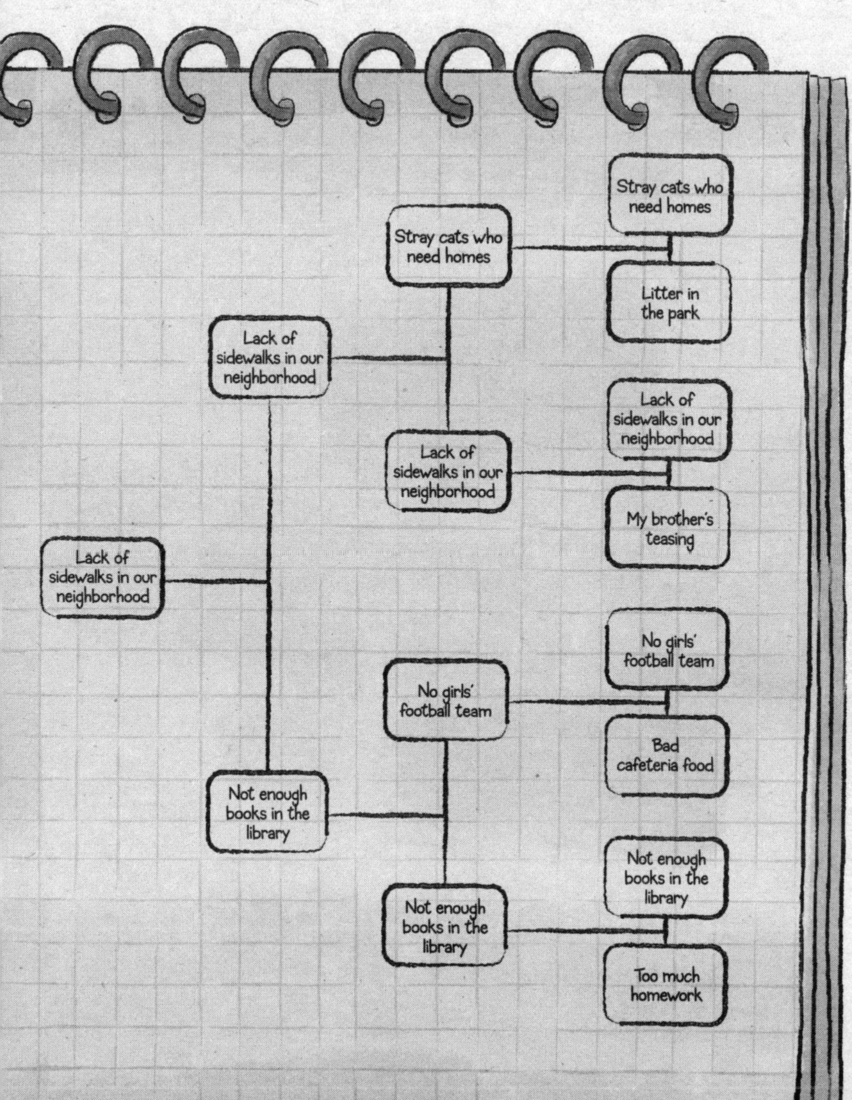

Journaling: Look Outside and Inside to Find Your Cause

Grab your journal and draw a bracket diagram like the one featured on the previous page.

Step 1) Fill in the boxes in the first column on the left.
Step 2) Fill in the boxes in the last column on the right.
Step 3) For each bracket, choose one.
Step 4) Continue until you have a final pair. Combine to create your Take Action project!

Or if you want to get creative in a different way, create a few drawings that answer:

- Identity: How do you see yourself?
- Interests: What's your favorite hobby or an activity that makes you feel great?
- Concerns: What do you care about and want to see changed?
- Community: What is your home or neighborhood like? Are your concerns being addressed by your community? In what ways, and what could be better?

Don't limit yourself to just a few sketches or notes. The more you draw or journal, the more ideas you may develop.

Identifying a Root Cause

The root cause of an issue centers on how it starts and why it continues. A root cause is an issue's source, and if you eliminate the factors or situations that activate the source, things will improve. For example, the root cause of the challenge the Girl Scouts faced was a lack of a sidewalk on a busy stretch of road. Without a sidewalk, people had an inability to bike safely from one part of town to another. Once the root cause (the lack of a sidewalk) was addressed, these issues went away. People could walk and bike with ease!

Here's another example of a root cause. Imagine that at your school, a lot of first graders go to the nurse's office right after recess with bruises and scrapes on their arms and legs. Many of these kids say it's because they tripped while running on the playground. You go to first-grade recess one day and notice that a lot of students have untied shoes. *Of course,* you think. *They're tripping on their shoelaces!* So, you decide to start a "Shoelace Club" every Thursday at recess, and you teach about thirty first graders how to tie their shoes. Within weeks, the nurse reports fewer bruises and scrapes.

It often helps to ask why to find the root cause. You may need to ask why as many as five times or more to peel back the layers of an issue, see the factors that contribute to it, and pinpoint the solution. For example:

First graders are getting injured at recess.
Why?
Because they are tripping.
Why?
Because their shoes are untied.
Why?
Because they don't know how to tie them.
Why?
Because they haven't learned yet.
My solution is to start Shoelace Club!

Sometimes finding a root cause may not be as easy as walking out to the playground to observe and ask why. In fact, you may have to talk to lots of people and do research to discover what's causing an issue.

These steps may guide you as you dig deep into the heart of an issue:

Ask people questions: Start with the people affected by this issue. Why do they think this issue is happening? How does it make them feel? When did it start? Have they ever experienced this issue somewhere else? Remember to really listen and be empathetic. People, organizations, or cultures are experts on their own needs. Don't assume that you understand what a community needs without asking.

Get ideas: This involves asking more questions! Ask the people affected by the issue what they would change or do if they could. Research what people or organizations are already doing or have done in the past in response to the issue. What worked for them and what didn't work? Which factors leading to the issue are you most interested in changing? You can also read about this issue throughout history. Go online and see if this has happened in other communities. Watch a movie or videos about it. Learning more about the root causes and background will help you understand why things are the way they are and what would be most helpful (and what wouldn't!) for the affected communities.

Observe: Look around your community (your local, national, or global community—or all of them!) and think about what you see. Is this issue being addressed anywhere? Do you see places where it's being ignored?

Throughout this process, you can still ask why again and again!

Whatever you discover when you're identifying the roots of an issue, know that not every issue has one single cause. A variety of factors can lead to issues within a community. While you may not be able to take action to change *all* of them, with a better understanding of the background and the people affected by an issue, you can get close.

She's Got This!

During the COVID-19 pandemic, a group of Girl Scouts learned the value of asking why to get to the root cause of an issue and find a solution.

The girls had frequently visited the elderly residents at their local retirement home. When COVID hit, however, visiting hours were cut off for everyone except immediate family members. The girls missed their elderly friends, so they kept in contact with the director of the facility, and she reported that the residents missed them, too.

This sadness was a big concern, and the girls

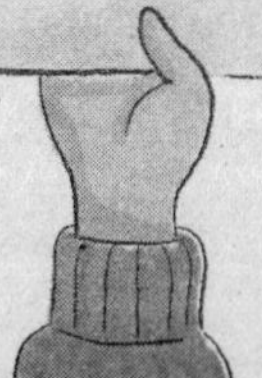

decided it needed a solution.

Although the root cause of the issue seemed obvious (there was a pandemic happening!) the girls still asked why.

Issue: The elderly residents are sad.

Why?

Because they miss their Girl Scout friends.

Why?

Because their friends make them happy.

Why?

Because their friends tell them about all the exciting things they're doing in school, do activities with them, and make the day feel shorter. Without interesting ideas and happenings that originate outside the retirement home, the days are *loooong*.

Root cause of sadness: There is nothing from "outside" to occupy the residents' imaginations.

The girls decided to collect toilet paper rolls, pine cones, and egg cartons to make bird feeder kits not just for their friends at the nearby retirement home, but for four other retirement homes as well! They even put together instruction sheets that explained the assembly for activities' directors at the retirement homes. The directors immediately reported that the residents loved the bird feeders because they made the residents feel connected to the outside world.

Just by asking why three times, they discovered a root cause they hadn't thought of—and they developed a way of helping.

Think About Resources and What's Realistic

You are smart and strong and have *really good* ideas, but making meaningful change isn't always the easiest thing to do. It's totally common to face limitations or constraints when you decide where and how you want to take action. For example, after Olympic fencer Ibtihaj Muhammad became the first Olympic athlete to wear a hijab in competition (and win a medal!) Ibtihaj used her influence to start a company that would make colorful, fashion-forward traditional dress for Muslim women. Ibtihaj didn't have an unlimited supply of money when she founded her clothing company, so she had to ask for financial help from her aunt and uncle. She also only had a few employees to help her, so she started out offering only ten designs, even though she dreamed of a *huge* brand with hundreds of styles. Ibtihaj dealt with her limitations, started small, and now her company sells products around the world.

Try not to let restrictions or limitations get you down. Asking for help, working within your means, and thinking about what's realistic are central parts of taking action. Remember, good things come to those who wait and work for it, so take the time to think about the resources you have on hand—and what you will need.

These resources include:

Supplies: What supplies do you have on hand? Are you going to need to go shopping for things? Can you ask others—like community members or even shop owners—to donate supplies?

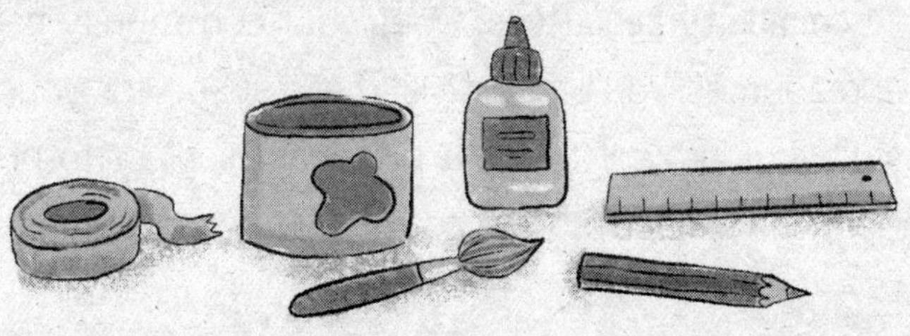

Money: Do you need to spend money on your project or activity? Where are you going to get that money? Just how much money do you think you'll need? How can you raise the funds?

Time: How much time is your service activity going to take? When can you do it? During the week or on weekends? How can you balance working on this project in addition to your other commitments and responsibilities? Will you still have enough time to recharge and spend time with your friends and family? You have to take care of your own needs, too!

Adult involvement: Will you need help on this project from a trusted adult? Do they have the interest and time to do so? Have you talked with them about your ideas?

Community resources: Does your community have the resources you'll need? Is there space for you to install your project (if it's a physical thing) or to hold meetings to discuss your project? For example, if you want to put a community fridge on your block to help people who need food, is there an electrical outlet available for use? Will the business near it or your block or community association let you use theirs?

Reach: What's the best way to reach the people you want to help? How can you do that? Should you use social media, meet people in person, or text or email people? Should you have a table outside your school asking people to volunteer to help you out? Do you want to reach out in more than one way? Who can help you?

If any potential dealbreakers come up—for example, you realize you're going to have to raise a lot more money than you expected—start asking why again. You may discover the root cause of what's limiting you, and then you can seek a solution. If you can't find your way around a lack of resources, you might want to explore a different issue that better fits your interests and limitations. Don't worry, there are many issues out there waiting for an amazing leader like you!

Journaling: Look at Your Resources and Needs

Grab your journal and write down the resources you have and the resources you'll need. You can copy the following table into your journal as a guide. The questions you might want to address are listed in the first column, but you may discover you have more (or fewer) areas you'll need to cover. Every project is different. If you have more than one issue you're considering, create this chart for each of them. This may help you decide which issue is the most realistic for you to tackle.

Potential Resources & Needs	What You Already Have	What You Need	Ideas for How You Can Get What You Need
Supplies: • What will you need? • What do you already have on hand? • Can people or businesses donate items you need?			
Money: • How much will these things cost? Ask an adult for help! • Do you need to raise funds or get donations?			
Time: • Write down your schedule and see where you have spare time. • How much time per week or day do you think your project will take? • Can you schedule that time into your calendar?			

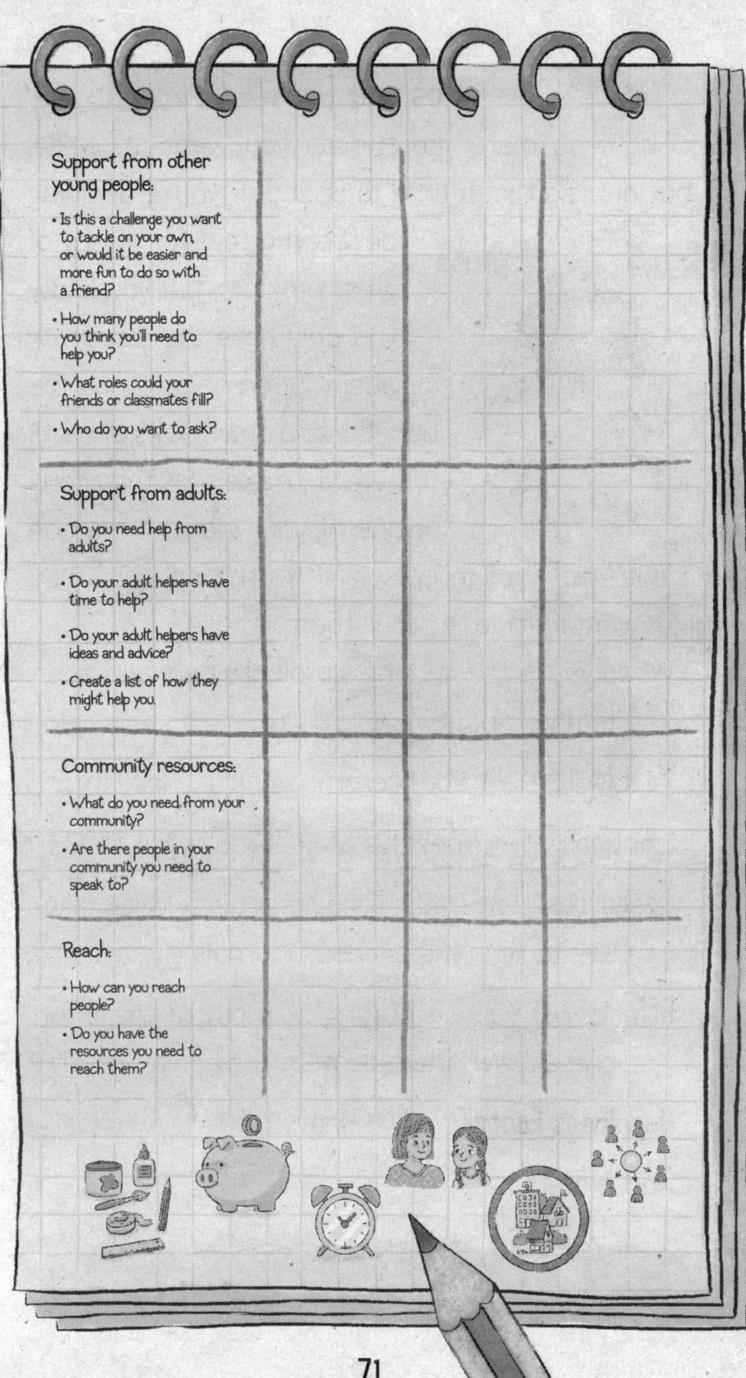

Support from other young people:
• Is this a challenge you want to tackle on your own, or would it be easier and more fun to do so with a friend?
• How many people do you think you'll need to help you?
• What roles could your friends or classmates fill?
• Who do you want to ask?
Support from adults:
• Do you need help from adults?
• Do your adult helpers have time to help?
• Do your adult helpers have ideas and advice?
• Create a list of how they might help you.
Community resources:
• What do you need from your community?
• Are there people in your community you need to speak to?
Reach:
• How can you reach people?
• Do you have the resources you need to reach them?

Pros and Cons

You have so many great ideas you want to tackle, but only so much time to spend! If you're deciding between a few (or a ton) of great projects, but you know you only have the resources for one, it often helps to list the benefits and drawbacks of each. If there are more pros than cons for one of your ideas, it may be the one you want to pursue. If it's the opposite, you might want to move on to something else.

When you're considering a project's pros and cons, be sure to think about:

Real Need: Does your community truly *need* this?

Emotions: How does this project make you feel?

Resources: How much time and energy will it take? (See table in the previous journaling activity.)

Effort: Will you be putting in most of the effort yourself? Will there be people who can help?

Happiness Factor: Will you have fun?

And more!

Journaling: Pros and Cons

Write all the pros and cons of your project ideas in your journal. Take time to think about them—more ideas and thoughts will probably come to you overnight or in a few days. If you like, you can create a journal entry that looks something like this:

	Idea #1 Pros	Idea #1 Cons	Idea #2 Pros	Idea #2 Cons
Real Needs				
Emotions				
Resources				
Work				
Happiness Factor				
Other				

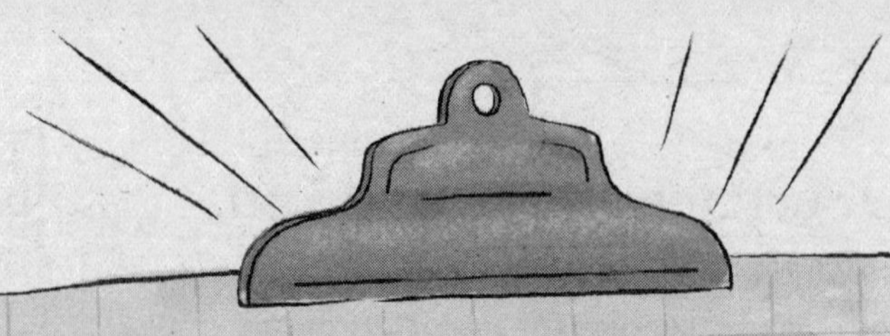

Take Action Tip: Let Life Happen

Sometimes people become so busy planning, thinking, and doing that they miss the beauty happening all around them. As you try to identify an issue you want to take action to help, stop sometimes and just be. Don't think so much. Don't make yourself too busy. Try to soak up the sights and smells around you, and your life will happen. Suddenly, you may discover an issue in the world you truly care about!

CHAPTER FOUR:

BUILD YOUR TEAM

You are so passionate, smart, and dedicated that you may think, *I can* definitely *make a positive change in the world all by myself!* Sure, you can, but it's not necessary! Much of the time, not only is it a lot easier to make a difference if you have a team, but you can also make a much bigger impact and have a lot more fun with friends by your side.

Look at some of the great athletes competing today, like Olympic gold-medal-winning soccer player and FIFA World Cup champion Alex Morgan and four-time WNBA champion and five-time Olympic gold-medal-winning basketball player Sue Bird. Both have teammates they depend on. Even an athlete who doesn't play a team sport, like US professional tennis sensation Coco Gauff, has coaches, trainers, doctors, and families cheering her on and helping her be the best athlete she can be. These friends, family members, coaches, teachers, and fans make up Coco's team, and they are all working toward the same goal.

If your goal is to take action and make a positive difference in the world, building a team is a part of the journey!

Build Your Dream Team—and Include Experts

It's time to gather your team!

Some teams are big and some are small, but their common thread is that they believe in the cause and are enlisted to help develop the solution. They want to help, not just *you*, but the community you're trying to impact. As you look for team members, keep your goal in mind. Is your team going to be willing to do the work and excited to make a solution happen?

The first people you probably think about having on your team are your friends, and that's understandable. Your besties are the people you're most comfortable being around, and you know them *so* well. You probably think that spending more time with them will be a nonstop party.

But try hard to be objective. Just because someone is your best friend doesn't mean they are the best person to join your team. If you want to take action and make a positive change, you need people who have special skills and interests that will help with that issue. Your BFF might be the most fun person in the world, but when you stop and think about it, maybe you already know she's kind of disorganized and is busy every afternoon doing gymnastics, which would conflict with the team meetings you were thinking of holding after school. Also, your team members should feel passionate—or at least interested—in your issue. Imagine you want to help the stray cat population in your neighborhood find safe places to live. If your BFF has a cat allergy, she might not be the best person for the job! She can support you and cheer you on, but others might be better for your core team.

Journaling: What Do You Need in a Team Member?

Before you think about what abilities and strengths you need from your team members, it's helpful to think about what *your* strengths are. Great team members often take up where you leave off and do things you can't or don't want to do. Grab your journal and write down your strengths. You can even consider making a list like this:

I'm Good At:

- Leading meetings
- Coming up with ideas
- Staying focused until a job is done

Now think about your limitations. Is there anyone out there who has an ability you don't have that you need for your team? What are those qualities? You might even try to use a table like this:

I Could Be Better at . . . Or I'm Not Interested In . . .	Someone Could Help Me With . . .	People I Could Ask
Taking notes and organizing	Keeping records, acting as a secretary	My sister's best friend, who is very organized
Sourcing resources we need, like money	Fundraising	The student government treasurer
Talking to new people	Being the voice of my organization to the outside world	My cousin who knows everyone and is very outgoing

When you're forming your team, it's also a good idea to reach out to people of different ages, races, beliefs, and more. Individuals who come from different backgrounds than you will probably have ideas you never would have thought of or suggestions that could improve your project. Are you trying to organize a fundraiser in your neighborhood, like a Girl Scout Cookie sale, or something else, and you want as many people as possible to pitch in? Someone who has familiarity with the large Yemeni population in your neighborhood might point out that you need to reach out to them, too. You notice that there's a Yemeni festival coming up in your town, so you reach out to the organizer to see if you can participate somehow to raise awareness for your fundraiser.

Having a diverse team will also help you challenge some of the assumptions you've made about the root causes you've uncovered or the details of your plan. For example, what if you assume that the senior citizens in your neighborhood won't want to race in the fun run you've planned? Having a senior citizen on your team might point out that many senior citizens love running, or that you could be more inclusive of people with mobility issues by making it a fun run *and* walk!

It's a great idea to seek the advice of experts, too, or to have a few on your team. "Expert" is a broad term, and it doesn't necessarily mean a "Subject Matter Expert" (SME), who is someone who holds a degree related to whatever cause you're championing or who has a job connected to your project. For example, if you are trying to help the stray cats near your home, it's not a requirement that you have a team member who has worked at a pet rescue.

However, an SME *can* be helpful. SMEs do have particular expertise, and they may be able to help you plan, find the right resources, and more. For example, chatting with a veterinarian you are friendly with may help you better understand the needs of stray cats. If you can't find an SME, though, that's okay! Just ask friends and advisers who can help you talk to people, research, ask why, and more.

She's Got This!

Cancer had been a big part of Lauren V.'s life: her mom and grandfather had suffered from it when she was little, and she'd recently lost a friend from her dance class to cancer. Her friend's death had hit her hard, but her courage had also inspired her. "She had so much spirit through the whole thing," Lauren said. "She didn't just exist or suffer through this incredibly painful experience . . . she actually danced through it."

Lauren wanted to give other people with cancer that same kind of hope, so she decided to create a book that would profile people living with cancer and offer their wisdom, advice, and experiences. She knew she'd have to do a lot of writing, so she asked herself if she knew any "writing experts." She did! Her school had a writing teacher, and she knew that teacher would challenge her, make her ask hard questions, and help her make a plan. Sure enough, the teacher was an amazing team member, and the book came out beautifully.

Recruit Volunteers

Now that you know what skills you need your team to have, it's time to find volunteers who are excited to help bring this project to life.

Before you start asking people, think about these things first:

How many volunteers do you need? You don't need to know an exact number, but it's a good idea to estimate. When you have too few volunteers, you may feel overwhelmed. If you have too many volunteers, and there's nothing for them to do, they might feel like their time is being wasted.

What are your needs? What do you need your volunteers do to? Brainstorm, talk to your team, and write down a list.

Engaging the Community

Once you have a strong team by your side, it's time to reach out even more. Engaging your community will bring awareness to your issue, help you find support for your cause, and make it easier to get to work when you're ready to put a plan into action. You may even meet more potential team members!

The thought of reaching out to your community about your cause might be a little intimidating at first, so if you feel any nerves, that's totally normal! Just remember that you have a team, and they are there to support you. You can also be confident in the knowledge that your cause is worthwhile (in fact, it's amazing!) and you are uniquely qualified to take action because you have so much passion in your heart.

You've got this!

Ways to Engage Your Community

There are so many ways you can connect with your community, from social media to going door-to-door to appearing on your local TV news (might as well aim high, right?). Below you'll find a checklist with a few ideas you can follow. Check off as many as you like and add a few of your own. Know that you don't have to do them all because every community is different and every project is unique.

- Put up signs around the neighborhood that explain the issue you care about. Be sure to include a way to contact you (like an email address), a website (if you've created one), or a social media site (if your project has one). Be sure not to put any personal information, like where you live, and be sure to have an adult review your signs. Your flyer could look like this:

◆ If your community has a social media site, or people frequently post on NextDoor, post something there. Be sure to ask an adult who has an account to help you.

- Put flyers in people's mailboxes.
- With an adult, go door to door. Introduce yourself, explain the issue you're working on, and hand them a flyer (if you have one—they are helpful!)

- Go to a neighborhood association meeting, such as a Parent-Teacher Association (PTA) meeting or Rotary meeting.
- Have an adult help you call the local television station to tell them about your cause. TV stations love stories about people like you making a difference.

- Enlist the support of community leaders or politicians. Usually they have email addresses, and it's actually their job to respond to members of their community.

Keep Your Team Motivated

Chances are that most people want to help you out because they care about the cause you're working for and are looking forward to the amazing results your team is going to achieve. But they also want to enjoy the work they're doing! While you're taking action to make the world a better place, don't forget to keep the fun alive. Motivating your team with positive energy will help them stay interested, invested, and happy. There are lots of ways you can drum up excitement about making a change, such as:

- Update your social media regularly with fun photos, updates, and inspirational messages.
- Send daily or weekly email updates to your team that include fun, motivating stories or exciting developments. Or just tell your team how much you love them!

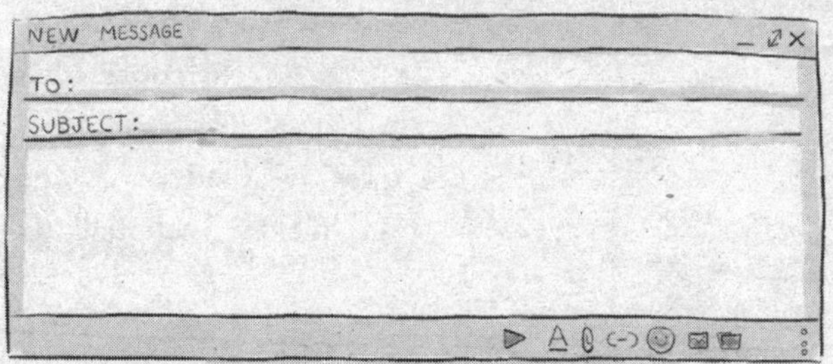

When you meet, use your time wisely (start and finish on time) and make it fun! Bring donuts, play music, and be sure to emphasize everyone's many strengths.

Take Action Tip: Game Time!

Games are another great way for everyone on your team to get to know each other and spark creativity. Here are some games that will help you break the ice and build a great team. Teams are all about community and building bridges, so these activities are collaborative rather than competitive. Remember, you are all working toward the same goal.

Blizzard: This game focuses on how to recognize everyone's strengths and talents. Gather each member of your team into a circle and give each a pencil and strip of paper. On the paper, each person should write down three of their strengths and talents. Then ball up

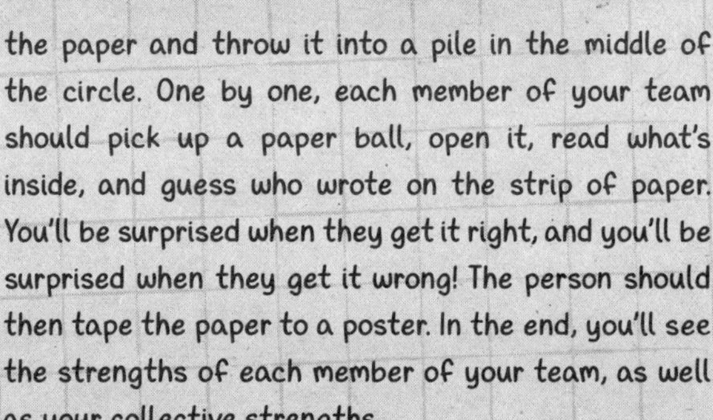

the paper and throw it into a pile in the middle of the circle. One by one, each member of your team should pick up a paper ball, open it, read what's inside, and guess who wrote on the strip of paper. You'll be surprised when they get it right, and you'll be surprised when they get it wrong! The person should then tape the paper to a poster. In the end, you'll see the strengths of each member of your team, as well as your collective strengths.

Musical Chairs: This is not the musical chairs you're probably used to, and you don't even need chairs to play, but it's an awesome way to recognize and celebrate what everyone on your team is great at. It can also keep your team and volunteers motivated, as well as make meetings fun! To play, form a circle with your teammates. All but one of your team members should sit down. The person left standing is the leader who calls out a strength or talent. The people who have that quality stand up and find a new place to sit. The leader automatically gets to sit. The person who doesn't sit fast enough is the new leader. In this game, no one wins in the traditional sense, but everyone wins because you get to recognize how amazing you all are!

CHAPTER FIVE:

PINPOINT YOUR GOAL

So what does it mean for something to be sustainable? You might have heard the term "sustainable" as it relates to the environment. Sustainability often means doing as little harm as possible to the earth so the planet can survive and thrive. These sustainable activities include using refillable water bottles instead of disposable ones, eating less meat, turning the lights off, recycling, and walking or biking rather than driving.

The kind of sustainable change you need to think about when you take action is similar. As it relates to making change, sustainability means the ability to help something (not just the Earth!) last for a long time. A sustainable solution asks: Will you have the resources, time, money, team, and support to make positive change stick? Is your solution a short-term one, or can it last months and years? And does the new path you've blazed take a community forward (in a constructive way) rather than keeping it the same or moving it backward? Is this something the community will be happy with for a long time?

Quiz: Sustainable Change Versus Short-Term Change

Can you tell the difference between sustainable change and short-term change?

1. There's a water shortage, called a drought, in your state that looks like it might last all summer.

   A. You convince your caregivers to stop watering the grass during the summer to conserve water. It will just grow back when it starts to rain, and who cares if your grass is green, anyway?

   B. You convince your family to replace the front lawn with a drought-resistant garden. Think of the water you'll save every year!

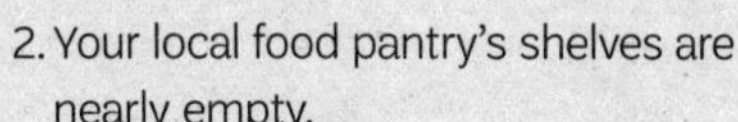

2. Your local food pantry's shelves are nearly empty.

   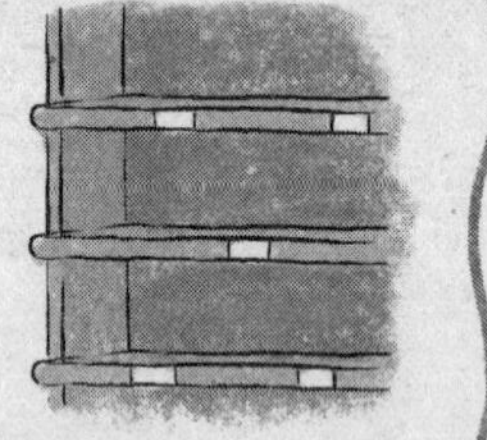

   A. Buy a bag of groceries to donate to the food pantry.

   B. Start a school club to host monthly food drives for the pantry and promote the club on social media.

3. There's a pond near your house that ducks swim in. People have picnics near the pond, then leave their trash, and it blows into the pond. You're worried about the ducks!
   - A. Pick up the trash every Sunday morning with your friends.
   - B. Put a trash can near the pond with a sign that says, "Trash Kills Ducks!" Then write your mayor and request a more permanent sign.

Answers

1. B, 2. B, 3. B

Three Paths to Creating Sustainable Change

How do you make change sustainable? It's simple! Here are three easy-to-follow paths you can follow to create sustainable change for a cause you believe in.

Make your solution long lasting: When you create a long-lasting solution, it sticks. It's not temporary, and it doesn't only last a day or a week. Sure, maybe it doesn't survive *forever* (what does?), but the change you make will be around for a long, long time. For example, a

long-lasting solution is the wildflower garden you urge your school to plant instead of grass. You know that the wildflowers will bloom every spring and summer year after year, and they won't be much effort for your biology teacher (who loves the idea!) to maintain. Because wildflowers require a lot less water than grass, they will help your school conserve water.

Educate and inspire others to be part of the change: A long-lasting solution may also be something that creates an impression on other people and makes them want to help change the world for the better, too. For example, imagine you start a club at your school that leads monthly diversity celebrations, such as Mental Health Awareness, Disability Pride, and Black History throughout the year. Chances are good everyone will have so much fun that the club will continue year after year. Maybe someone in your class will even ask if they can help you recruit speakers to talk to the entire school at assembly about diversity and inclusion. Just like that, you started a movement! You initiated an inspiring change that made a big impression on other people. People will be talking about your club and its events for years, saying how they really brought the community together.

She's Got This!

A group of Girl Scouts created sustainable change when they developed a solution that educated and inspired their classmates. These girls noticed that a lot of their peers brought plastic water bottles to school every day. This concerned them because they'd heard that 86 percent of plastic water bottles end up in landfills in the United States every year, and that water bottle manufacturing releases 2.5 million tons of pollution into the atmosphere.

They knew this had to stop. So they decided to convince others to use reusable water bottles. They hung up signs around the rooms that showcased all the negative effects of plastic water bottles, and they created charts that showed what percentage of students in each class had gotten rid of their disposable

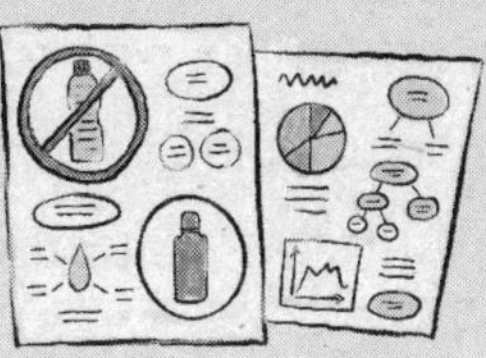

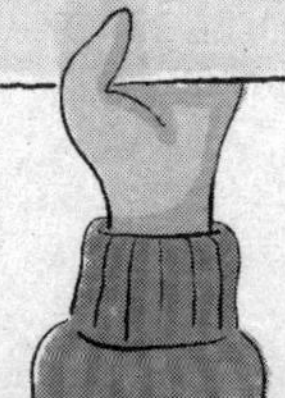

bottles. Soon their movement spread to the whole school. They even gave a presentation at the school assembly! Their efforts inspired many students, teachers, and other members of their school community to use reusable water bottles instead of plastic water bottles, not just that year, but beyond. It was the first school-wide green initiative in their school's history, and it all started with one group of girls taking action.

Change a rule, regulation, or law: When you help change a rule, regulation, or law, you are making sustainable change. There are so many kinds of rules—big or small—that you can influence. You could convince your student council or principal's office to enact a rule that says that no one can use plastic water bottles anymore. (And perhaps you start a fund to supply reusable water bottles to the whole school.) These rules, regulations, or laws can be in communities as small as your neighborhood or friend group or as big as the whole planet! No change is too small if it makes the world a better place.

She's Got This!

When she was fifteen, Cassie Levesque was shocked to learn that, across the country, child marriage—meaning kids under the age of eighteen being married off to older adults—was still happening in the United States. Cassie knew that both her grandma and great-grandma had been child brides, but that was long ago, right? Nope. Even in her home state of New Hampshire, kids as young as thirteen were allowed to get married. For her Girl Scout Gold Award project, the highest award in Girl Scouting, she decided to work to raise the required age of marriage in her state. She met a lot of resistance along the way, including from a state senator who said that he would never change a law "on the basis of a request from a minor doing a Girl Scout project." In 2018, Cassie stood by the New Hampshire governor as he signed a bill into

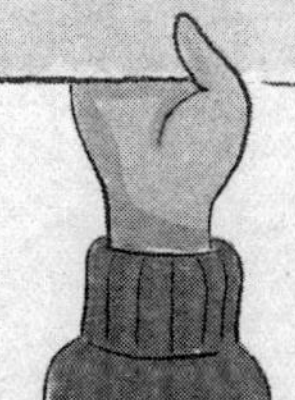

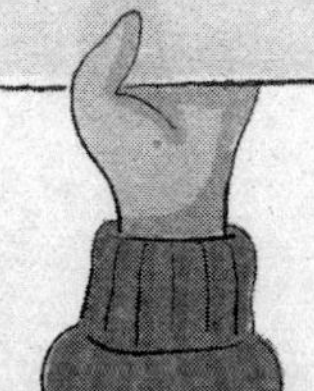

law raising the minimum marriage age to sixteen. Cassie immediately set her sights higher, and when she was nineteen, she ran for the New Hampshire House of Representatives—and won! She has vowed never to stop fighting for a law that will raise the minimum age to eighteen, when young people legally become adults.

Fourteen Ideas for Sustainable Solutions

To help you come up with ideas about how to make sustainable change, here are some ideas of projects you can tackle and ways you can go about making a difference. Just remember that while the suggestions below can be amazing additions to your community, your community has to *need* and *want* them. If you see a need for an improvement, others may not, so be sure to research the needs of the people you want to impact (see Chapter Three for more on how to do this). In addition, make sure you have the resources and a solid plan to maintain these solutions (for more on resources, see Chapter Three).

Make Your Solution Long Lasting

1. Create and install something outside (birdhouses, dog run, community fridge, ropes course, sensory trail for children with disabilities, etc.). Collaborate with the local Department of Public Works to set up a plan to maintain the installation.
2. Make and install something inside (Maker Space, reading room, computer lab, etc.). Talk with the building's management to plan how to maintain the installation.

3. Create a collection (donate children's books to the children's hospital or family shelter, create audio oral histories for town museum, etc.). Collaborate with the organization's management to determine how to maintain the collection.
4. Advocate for building infrastructure that benefits the community (sidewalk, bridge, park, streetlights, stoplight, etc.). Collaborate with the local Department of Public Works to come up with a maintenance plan.

Educate and Inspire Others to Be Part of the Change

5. Make a "how to help" handout. Pass it out to your community members and/or post it on your community message board or website.

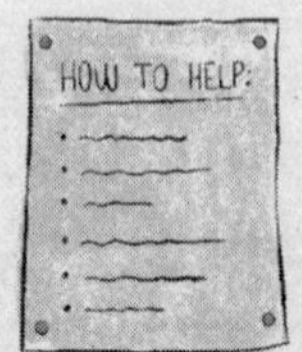

6. Give a speech at a school assembly or at a town event.
7. Write and perform a song about your issue, then make a music video and post it online. Promote your video by emailing friends and family (and asking your peers to do so as well), post it on social media, and—if possible—engage the interest of the local press.

8. Create a workshop (perhaps in partnership with a local business or organization) to teach a skill that helps solve the root of your issue. That could be anything, such as coding, camping, canoeing, robotics, sewing, car care, healthy eating, gardening, home repair, budgeting, etc.
9. Create a social media campaign to spread awareness.
10. Make a "playbook" to help others follow your lead (how to mentor

robotics teams, organize a workshop or event, advocate to the city council, create an online petition, change a law, etc.).

Change a Rule, Regulation, or Law

11. Make a presentation to your school principal.
12. Speak up at your representative's town hall or city council meeting—you almost always have to sign up in advance, but there are usually no age restrictions.
13. Create an online petition.
14. Contact your local elected officials to talk about a law you'd like to see in your area, or to discuss one that you disagree with.

The Five Elements of a Great Solution

Sustainable is one of five elements of a great solution that will make a difference for a long, long time. A great solution is also Deep, Doable, Positive, and Empowering! It changes people's lives—and the world! That's all because of you!

As you decide on a sustainable solution for an issue you care about, also think about:

Does it have depth? In terms of taking action, depth means that it doesn't just tackle an issue on its surface. It goes *deep into the heart* of the issue. To do this, a great solution addresses people's real needs and focuses on the causes of concerns. For example, pretend that the issue you care about is the fact that people are constantly writing or drawing graffiti on the ugly green wall outside your cafeteria. *I know what to do*, you think. *I'll just get a washrag and some soap and wash it off every day.* Nope. That solution has no depth because it doesn't address *why* people are writing on the wall, nor does it stop people from wanting to write on the wall in the first place. You ask why and learn that people write on the wall because it's become a bit of a tradition, and people have stopped viewing the wall as school property. "A kid wrote on the wall once, so we all started doing it," one person said. "I know it's bad, but that wall is ugly, and everyone writes on it." Consider a solution like this: With the permission

of your principal, create a club to design and paint an awesome mural over the ugly green wall. Invite some of the kids who'd been drawing on the wall when they weren't supposed to—clearly they like making public art! Then hold an assembly to unveil the new mural. Your fellow students will feel a sense of pride seeing their work on display and begin to value the wall as school property and choose not to ruin it. Presto! This great solution addresses the cause (people stopped caring about school property because they didn't see its value) and anticipates people's needs (they want a colorful, happy-looking school).

She's Got This!

At nine years old, a Girl Scout was diagnosed with cancer. Being in the hospital for chemotherapy was hard for her because she felt sick and hated missing out on school and her Girl Scout meetings. But what was equally hard was how lonely she felt. She'd have chemo during the day, and in the middle of the night she'd wake up sick and scared. When she'd get up in the morning, she wished she felt well enough to walk down the hospital hallway so she could talk to another patient who was going through what she was.

She wasn't sure what to do, so she asked herself these questions:

What's the issue? Kids with cancer (like me) get lonely.

Why? Because getting treatment gets in the way of doing the things we normally do with the people we love and meeting people who are experiencing the same things we are.

How can I fix this? Give kids undergoing cancer treatment a way to prevent loneliness and help fix it when it creeps up.

When she felt well enough, this Girl Scout started an organization called Chat with Champs that raises money to put walkie-talkies in the rooms of

kids undergoing cancer treatment at Rady Children's Hospital in San Diego. The children in Rady's cancer wing can now talk to each other from their beds, sharing their questions, hopes, and fears—even in the middle of the night!

Is your solution doable or difficult? The best solutions are simple to put into action, won't take up all of your time, and are easy to follow for everyone. Basically, great solutions are things you don't really have to think about too much after you've put them into place. Imagine that your issue is all the trash that's been piling up in your local playground. All that garbage is gross to look at, possibly dangerous for the wild animal population, attracts too many bugs, and is ruining the good experience you and your friends have every day after school. You decide that your solution is to recruit a group of people to meet every Saturday at six a.m. to pick up the trash. All you have to do is find those people, create spreadsheets and signups, make sure everyone has the proper supplies to pick up the garbage every morning, and remember to set your alarm. Oh! And you need to find a place to store all the rubber gloves and rakes you need to buy. That's a lot of work! In fact, it's probably too much work for one person (and let's face it, nobody wants to be at the park every Saturday at six a.m.!). You need a simpler solution. Maybe you can consider advocating for your town to install a few more trash cans instead?

Activity: Is My Solution Super Doable or Really Difficult?

If you're trying to figure out if the solution you're considering is more difficult than it needs to be, start by considering your resources (see Chapter Three). After you've done that, check in with yourself and ask how you're feeling. The following quiz will help you figure out whether your solution is just right for you.

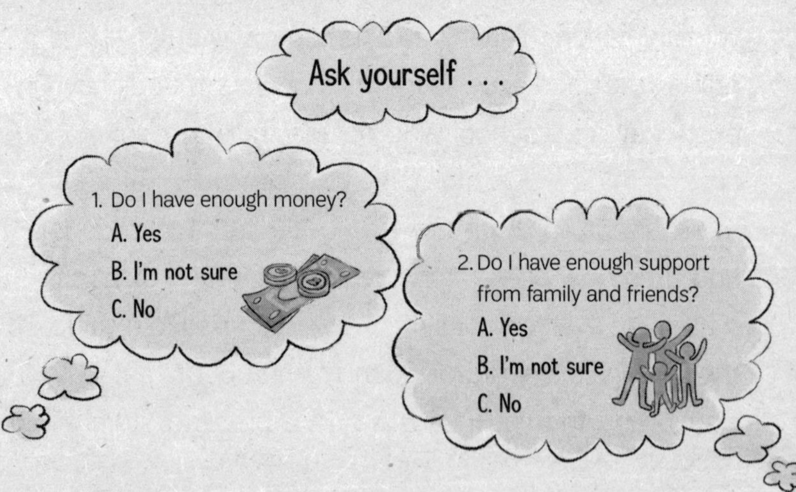

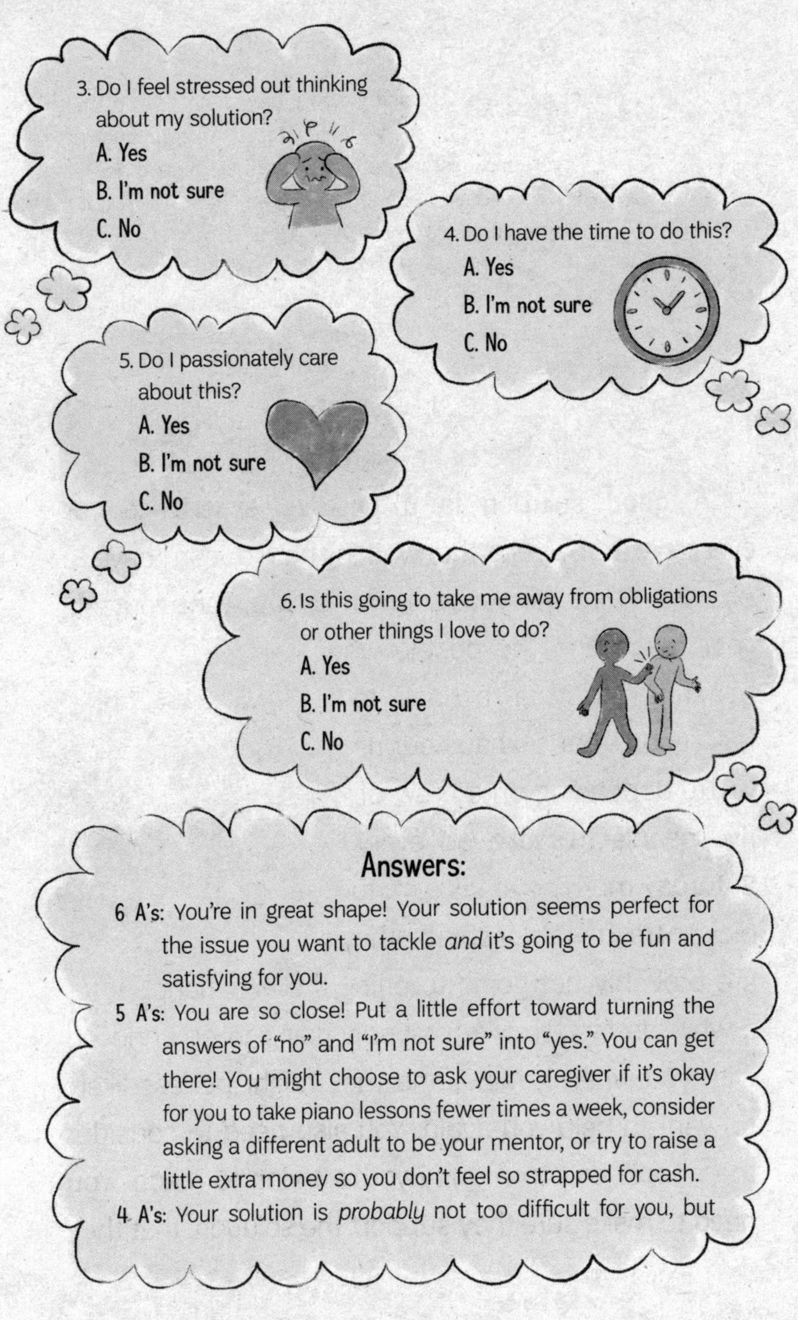

Answers:

6 A's: You're in great shape! Your solution seems perfect for the issue you want to tackle *and* it's going to be fun and satisfying for you.

5 A's: You are so close! Put a little effort toward turning the answers of "no" and "I'm not sure" into "yes." You can get there! You might choose to ask your caregiver if it's okay for you to take piano lessons fewer times a week, consider asking a different adult to be your mentor, or try to raise a little extra money so you don't feel so strapped for cash.

4 A's: Your solution is *probably* not too difficult for you, but you're going to have to double down and work harder than necessary to shore up your resources. Talk to an adult and see how you can raise more money or find more time. Maybe you even need to bring a partner on board so you can share the work fifty/fifty.

3 or fewer A's: It's unfortunately time to think of another solution. Don't worry, you will come up with something! You just need to reevaluate your time, passions, money, and other resources to see what that better solution is.

A good solution is a positive experience for everyone: Remember that working hard doesn't have to *be* hard. Whatever your solution is, you want yourself, your team, and the people who benefit from your actions to feel good—not exhausted! If you're depending on a crew of five people to wake up every Saturday morning at six a.m. to pick up trash—rain or shine—they are probably not going to enjoy the experience after a while. In fact, they're probably going to be annoyed with you when it rains, and they might be less likely to want to help you again. You also need to consider the people or community you're trying to reach. You need to make sure they support the solution, that they

can benefit from it easily, and that it won't require a lot of additional time or energy from them. For example, when the Girl Scout raised funds for the walkie-talkies that kids with cancer at Rady Children's Hospital in San Diego would use, she thought a lot about what their experience would involve. She wanted these patients' connections with others to be simple and immediate: no dialing or texting, no leaving voice mails, and no waiting for the three dots on a screen to turn into an answer. When you're in a hospital bed all alone, you want a simple, fast connection with someone, and a walkie-talkie gives that kind of positive experience. Guess what? Her solution worked! When she used one of the walkie-talkies during a stay in the hospital, she said how great it was because, "I got to meet other kids instead of just sitting in my bed watching TV."

A good solution empowers people: Maybe you've heard the famous saying, "If you give a person a fish, you feed them for a day. If you teach a person to fish, you feed them for a lifetime." What that means is that if your solution gives people *the tools to help themselves in the long term,* they will have the power to make better

lives on their own terms. A great solution doesn't treat people like they're helpless; it shows them that they have the power to help themselves. For example, if you advocated for and secured permanent trash cans for your local playground, you gave the people who use the playground an easier way to clean up after themselves. You gave *them* the tools to make their community a better place.

Quiz: Evaluating Solutions

Let's look at some of the issues girls around the world have tackled and how their solutions—and the steps they undertook to get to those solutions—check at least one of the boxes for a good solution. The first two issues are made-up examples, while the last two are real-life stories.

Issue 1: Adults often run their engines outside your school as they wait to pick up or drop off their children, which pollutes the air.

Solution 1: Stand outside the pickup/drop-off line and distribute flyers about how bad car exhaust is for the environment.

- **A.** Makes a change long lasting.
- **B.** Educates and inspires others to be part of the change.
- **C.** Changes a rule, regulation, or law.

Solution 2: Make a presentation to the school board or administrators why this is a concern and suggest a new rule that makes the pickup/drop-off area a "no idling" zone.

A. Makes a change long lasting.
B. Educates and inspires others to be part of the change.
C. Changes a rule, regulation, or law.

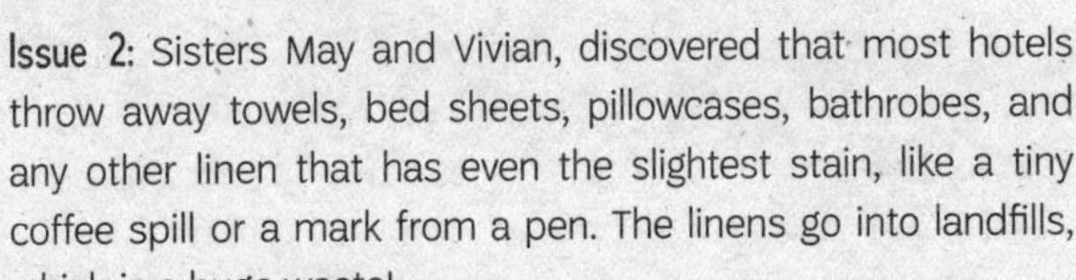

Issue 2: Sisters May and Vivian, discovered that most hotels throw away towels, bed sheets, pillowcases, bathrobes, and any other linen that has even the slightest stain, like a tiny coffee spill or a mark from a pen. The linens go into landfills, which is a huge waste!

Solution 1: Start an organization that collects these "imperfect" sheets and towels from nearby hotels and donate them to homeless shelters, pet rescues, and more.

A. Makes a change long lasting.
B. Educates and inspires others to be part of the change.
C. Changes a rule, regulation, or law.

Solution 2: Recruit and train volunteers to organize their own pickups at local hotels, then show how they can deliver them to organizations in need.

A. Makes a change long lasting.
B. Educates and inspires others to be part of the change.
C. Changes a rule, regulation, or law.

May and Vivian are still taking action! Their charitable organization has collected and delivered 30,000 linens, has helped 1,000 shelter residents, and has trained 30 chapters in 15 countries around the world.

Issue 3: After Taylor Richardson read Dr. Mae Jemison's book, *Find Where the Wind Goes*, her passion for space travel soared. It led her to raise funds to send herself to space camp at nine years old. She had fun but had mixed feelings about being the only Black girl there. She decided to help ensure more girls of color knew about camp and could attend.

Solution 1: Create opportunities for girls of color to be included in STEAM education.

A. Makes a change long lasting.

B. Educates and inspires others to be part of the change.

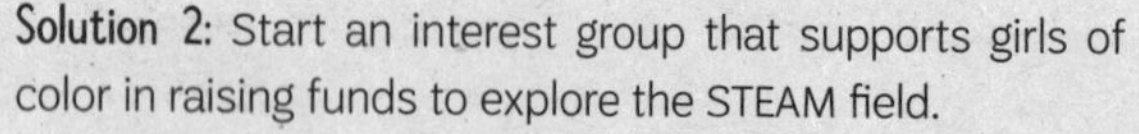

C. Changes a rule, regulation, or law.

Solution 2: Start an interest group that supports girls of color in raising funds to explore the STEAM field.

A. Makes a change long lasting.

B. Educates and inspires others to be part of the change.

C. Changes a rule, regulation, or law.

Taylor is also known for her award-winning documentary titled after her nickname, *Astronaut Starbright: The story of a young STEM advocate.* In the time since space camp she has raised more than $325,000 to introduce young girls of color to science with scholarships to space camps, STEAM book drives, and free tickets to science related movies like *Hidden Figures* As Taylor said, "Other girls need to know they can be astronauts."

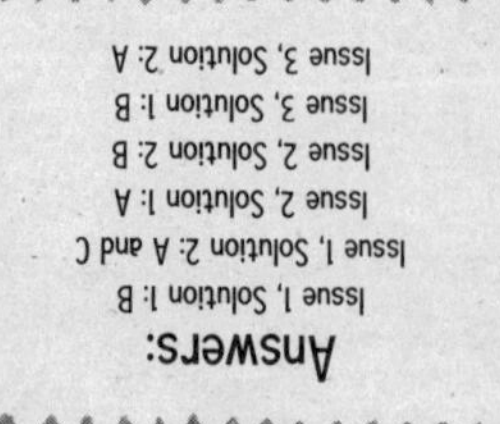

Answers:

Issue 1, Solution 1: B
Issue 1, Solution 2: A and C
Issue 2, Solution 1: A
Issue 2, Solution 2: B
Issue 3, Solution 1: B
Issue 3, Solution 2: A

Take Action Tip: Invest in People

People are the most sustainable resource you have! If you invest in people and take the time to empower them, you will have a true solution that lasts a lifetime. Even better, empowering people helps them become change-makers and builds community!

One Girl Scout learned this lesson firsthand when she decided to take action to help people in her community learn English. Lots of middle school students in her town speak English as a second language, and she realized this was an issue because most businesses and organizations in her community use English exclusively. She and her friends started a group called "Valor Para Todos," or "Value for All." Their plan was to meet throughout the year with a group of about a dozen sixth, seventh, and eighth graders to help them improve their English language skills.

The Girl Scout realized, however, that she could build community and empower her fellow middle schoolers if they would help *her* learn common Spanish phrases at the same time she helped *them* become more fluent in English. So, in each Valor Para Todos meeting, the two groups did homework, played games, and practiced speaking each other's languages. This element of exchange was super important to her mission of making sure everyone was involved, valued, and given opportunities to grow.

CHAPTER SIX:

CHECK YOURSELF

Before you get to the next step for taking action, it's important to check in with yourself and catch any biases that might get in the way of developing the best solution for the issue you're tackling.

But what's a bias? A bias is a belief or value system you hold in favor or against someone or something. Usually, that belief isn't right or fair. For example, if you join the basketball team and are six inches shorter than the rest of your teammates, they might have a bias against you, believing you won't be able to make a basket. They might not pass you the ball because of this bias. Their beliefs, or biases, are unfair. Throughout US history—and even today, though many communities are fighting against them—biases have existed against people, such as those with learning differences, the elderly, and women and girls.

These beliefs aren't just harmless thoughts. People who experience discrimination often face challenges that can affect life opportunities, how much money they can make, and even their mental health. A bias doesn't have to be a prejudice someone *wants* to believe. Your teammates might really love having you on the basketball team and feel bad about doubting your abilities, but they've just always thought that tall basketball players are better.

Someone may also hold a bias and be unaware of it. For example, some children might be disciplined unfairly because of their race. According to the American Psychological Association, Black children are often disciplined more harshly in schools than white students. This is shown to hurt future academic achievement, so it's really important to increase awareness around unconscious bias. Unintentional negative behaviors and mindsets can be learned in society from family or even friends, but it's up to everyone to treat all people with fairness and respect.

Quiz: Bias or No Bias?

See if you can spot the situations or thoughts driven by bias. Hint: it may be an unconscious bias.

Your new teacher is so pretty. You think, *She's going to be wonderful!*

You see an unhoused man on the street and worry that you're in an unsafe neighborhood.

Everyone in your class wants to watch a movie you've never heard of when there's a substitute. You think, *It must be a good movie if they all like it.*

You think your best friend stole something out of your locker. She swears she didn't, and you have no proof that she did. But you still don't trust her.

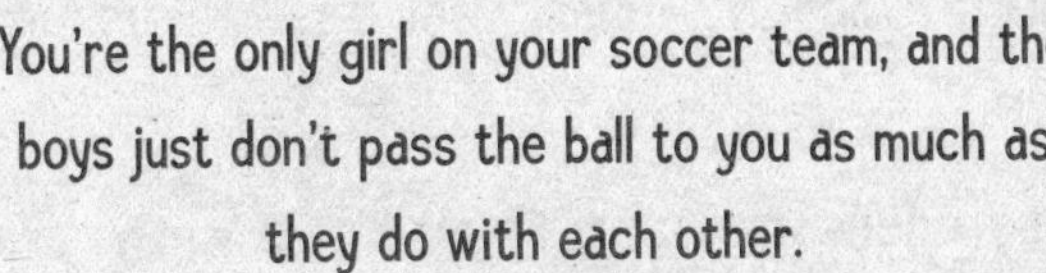

You're the only girl on your soccer team, and the boys just don't pass the ball to you as much as they do with each other.

Answer:

All of these are examples of bias! Here's how:

Shows a bias toward pretty people.

Shows a bias against unhoused people.

If you think "something must be good because everyone likes it," it shows a bias toward popular things.

Shows a bias based on suspicion and untruth

Shows a bias against girls in athletics.

Do you remember the Girl Scout troop from Chapter Two who learned about the lives of refugees and then welcomed them to their area? When they first started their project, they had all kinds of biases! They even held biases they didn't know about until they really stopped to think about them (again, these are called "unconscious biases"). In order to help the refugee community, they needed to question their beliefs and challenge their assumptions about their new neighbors. Some of these beliefs and assumptions included:

All refugees are poor: They're not! Many people are forced to leave their country because of dangerous conditions like war. They are people who make daily contributions to their communities as professionals working in business, education, and the medical field.

All refugees are happy to be in America because it's such an awesome place to live: That's not always true! A lot of refugees miss their countries terribly. After all, many didn't leave their country because they wanted to, they left because they had no other choice.

All refugees are different than you and me: Not true.

In fact, many girls in the troop had relatives, neighbors, and friends who fled their countries because of near-impossible living conditions. They had hopes and dreams about building a great life for their families. It's just that tough times caused them to need help resettling in a new place until conditions improved in their home countries.

The assumptions the girls made are biases. Biases would have affected the girls' plans if they hadn't educated themselves about the needs of the refugees and hadn't taken the time to research their backgrounds, history, and needs. Luckily, the troop checked their biases and were able to affect the refugees' lives in a positive, helpful way.

You're capable of doing that, too!

Who Has Biases?

The truth is, everyone does! Holding biases is very common. Often you're not even aware you have them. If you grow up in a community where people share similar identities, such as race and socioeconomic status, people who have different identities may be looked at in a negative way. Or if a relative or someone else you look up to has told you that certain types of people are bad, you may have believed them because you didn't know better. The adults we love and trust sometimes have biases, too!

But even if your community isn't very diverse, the *world* is diverse, so we have to fight our biases. Remember: we live in a global community, and we should strive to be global citizens. Believing someone isn't as good as you, might hurt you, or isn't as smart as you just because they are different than you isn't fair to them, and actually keeps you from meeting cool new people and expanding your world. Biases hurt everybody, so it's important that we open our minds and ask ourselves if we're being fair or making assumptions based on biases.

Journaling: How to Challenge Your Biases

There are some great questions to ask yourself when you meet another person so you don't accidentally hold a bias against them. These questions will help you examine your assumptions, slow down your decision making, and look for things you have in common rather than your differences.

Ask Yourself:

- What are two things I can learn about this person as an individual?
- What can I share about myself that will help us to get to know each other?
- Are there things I assume to know about them that are not facts? Where did those assumptions come from?
- What do I like about this person?

Journal about or think about these things, and, before you know it, you might feel like you've known the other person your whole life. Instead of worrying about your differences, you'll be trying to get to know them better.

How Biases Cause Issues

Biases can harm people and communities in all kinds of big and small ways. For example, imagine if Claire

S., who worked to put Holocaust education in schools, had assumed that older people aren't interested in the same things that young people are (this is called "Age Bias"). She would have missed the opportunity to become friends with Alter *and* help pass a very important law. If Alter had acted on Age Bias and assumed that young people only care about social media or shopping, the same would have happened to him.

Biases also:

Limit opportunities: Did you know that, according to data compiled by TeamStage, even though women account for 50.04 percent of the US workforce, only 27.1 percent of managers or company leaders are women? Did you also know that women are typically paid less than men for the *exact same work*? This pay gap and lack of opportunity doesn't just hurt grown women, it hurts girls, too, because they don't always see a place for themselves in the workforce or have role models for the kinds of jobs they're interested in. Without mentors or women they can look up to it's harder to make your dreams come true. The truth is that there's gender bias in the workplace, and women have a harder time making good money and advancing simply because of the biases against them.

Cause you to make unwise decisions: When you're biased against someone without getting to know them, you miss out on what they have to offer. What if they have similar interests as you do? If you got to know them, maybe you would've realized you wanted to be friends. Maybe they have talents or skills you could learn from, and maybe they'd want to learn from you, too.

Cause physical or emotional harm: In 2021, violence against Asians in the United States increased by 339 percent according to the Center for the Study of Hate and Extremism. Officials believe this was directly related to incorrect beliefs that Chinese people were responsible for the COVID-19 pandemic. In addition to the Asian American Pacific Islander (AAPI) community, the Black, Jewish, Latinx, LGBTQ+ communities—and many others—are victims of crimes because of bias. People can cause physical and emotional harm to others based on their race, religion, sexual orientation, and gender. Biases are horrible, but when we work to fight them, we can make the world a better place and do a better job of helping others.

She's Got This!

When a group of Girl Scouts were personally affected by religious bias against their Muslim identity, they decided to take action and do something about it.

Their school was connected to an Islamic Mosque that had received threats and witnessed groups of angry protestors gathered in front. These events made the girls—and the entire Islamic community they lived among—feel unsafe. When three Muslim students were killed, the girls became even more afraid. "People have heard terrible things about us. There are rumors that we do bad things and hurt people," said one of the girls. "But that's not true—it's not who we are."

The girls created a video called *Get to Know Me* to show how Muslims and people of other faiths are more similar than some might think. They showed a variety of people—all of whom are Muslim—holding

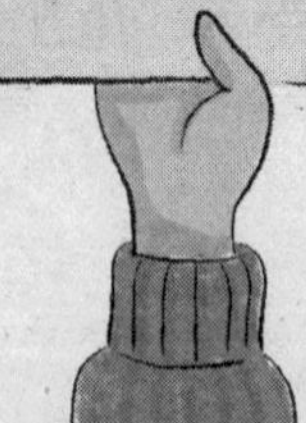

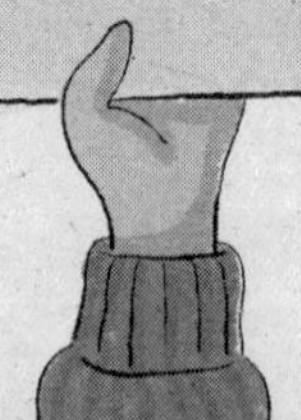

signs that explain the values of kindness, charity, and respect Islam has taught them. Then they decided to double their efforts by opening the doors of their mosque and inviting members of their community to tour it.

Increasing understanding across communities is an amazing way to create change. Before the event, the girls felt worried that people would use the day as an opportunity to protest or even destroy their mosque, but in the end, people were excited to attend and learn about their Muslim neighbors. So many people lined up to enjoy the day and explore the mosque that they decided to hold a second open house a few months later.

By educating others and causing people to question their biases, these girls broke down barriers and made a difference within their community.

How to Check Your Biases

Checking your biases means identifying and challenging the ideas and prejudices you may have about or against a person or community. We all have some biases—it's not a good thing, but it's true—but we also all have the power to change them and eventually get rid of them entirely! Now, no one expects you to go back in time and wipe away all the impressions and prejudices you absorbed when you were too young to walk or talk. But there *are* ways to remind yourself that—whether you realize it or not—you are constantly making assumptions about others that may affect them *and* yourself. When you check your biases, you can look at a situation with clear eyes, seeing it for what it is rather than what it isn't.

Here's how you can do that:

Educate yourself: When you don't understand someone's background or beliefs, you might feel unsure about them or even afraid. Some people assume Muslim people are dangerous, but have those people actually *met* Muslim people? Do they understand the peaceful beliefs of Islam? By learning about Islam and meeting Muslim people, a person with a bias can change their heart and mind.

Slow down and think things through: Unfortunately, humans are hardwired to have biases because the brain makes an immediate assumption about something. It's what you *do* with your bias that matters.

Slow down, don't make a decision right away, and then ask yourself some questions. When you take the time to be thoughtful and act with purpose, you can make unbiased decisions and take action in a way that doesn't impose your beliefs on others.

Surround yourself with people who are different than you: This is another form of education! Getting to know people who don't look like you, come from different backgrounds, have more or less money than you, or who have different values and beliefs is an awesome way to learn about the world, see things differently, and simply make new friends. There are so many ways you can do this. Sit at a new table at lunch. Read books and watch videos by and about people who do not look like you or come from different parts of the world. Join a new club or activity to meet people outside of your immediate circle. Can you think of any other places you may have the opportunity to spend time with people who aren't exactly like you?

Shift your perspective: A lot of times when we meet another person, we think about how different they are than us. Differences can be really interesting, so your brain tends to focus on them. Instead, force yourself to think about what you have in common. Do you both like the same music? Are you both into the same book series? Maybe you're in the same gym class at school. Take the time to notice these things and bond!

Think about facts: Always focus on the things you know about someone rather than assumptions or opinions. You may even have to write these down. When faced with facts, people often change their opinions. For example, when people walked into the Girl Scouts' open house at the mosque, they didn't see messages of hate. They witnessed beautiful crafts and words of peace and love. Those were facts, not opinions!

Facts are true statements that can be verified with evidence. Opinions are beliefs. For example, mermaids and unicorns are both mythical creatures; however, you may hold the opinion that mermaids are the coolest!

Journaling: Think About Your Biases

It's time to dig deeply into your life and think about the biases you might hold against people. Part of becoming a global citizen is shifting the way you think about your community, the world, and the people in it, so it can be really important to acknowledge the assumptions and opinions you have. Having a bias doesn't make you a bad person, but checking your biases and working to change them helps you to be a good one.

Open your journal and write down some of the times you may have held a bias against or toward someone, or a time you saw someone you care about acting on a bias. How did that affect your decision making? How did that change your relationship with that person? If you had to go back in time, would you do anything differently or say something different?

If you want, you can choose one situation to write about. Turn it into a story or a poem and illustrate it if you're inspired to.

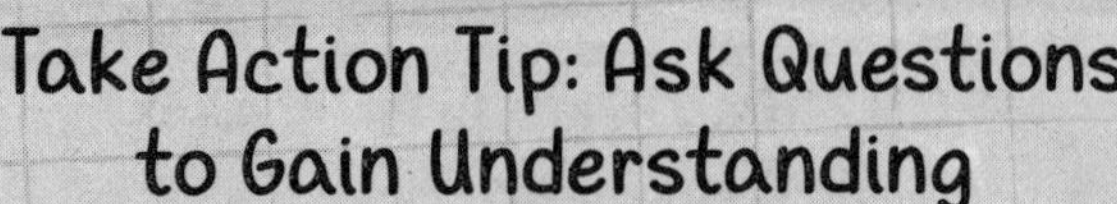

Take Action Tip: Ask Questions to Gain Understanding

When you are developing a solution—especially for a community you're not part of—it's important to meet their needs on their terms rather than yours. A good way to gain that understanding is to ask questions. This will also help you exercise your empathy muscles and check your biases. Ask yourself these questions:

- Have I done the proper research through written sources, online content, or experts on issues of bias?
- Have I asked people who would be impacted by my project if the solution I'm proposing is helpful?
- Could I involve others who are well informed to help me improve the impact of my project?
- What perspectives and voices do I need to include to make sure I represent all communities involved in the most respectful way?

Once you've answered those questions, you are well on your way to developing empathy, checking your biases, and creating a solution that empowers people and meets their needs. If you answered no to any of these questions, go back and work with the people you want to help. You'll have all yeses in no time!

CHAPTER SEVEN:

MAKE GOALS AND PLANS

You've identified a solution, and you've built a team full of volunteers, experts, and people who are as excited about making a difference as you are. You are well on your way to changing your community—and the world! But in order to make your dream solution a reality, you'll need goals and a detailed plan.

A goal is a way to evaluate your solution, letting you know that you are making progress toward it. For example, while Ibtihaj Muhammad's solution was to

make fashionable clothing for Muslim women, one of her goals might have been to design five dresses in her first month of business. You may have many goals when you take action, and that's fine; they are benchmarks along the path to your solution.

Next, a good plan will help you meet your goal or goals. Now, making a plan may be fun for you if you are super-organized and like to plot out your schedule on paper or in a planner with color coding and stickers. But it might be new for you if you like to go where the wind carries you. Pizza on Friday after the softball game? Maybe. You can't commit just yet.

Plans can be tailored for all kinds of leaders and all kinds of projects. So no matter which type of planner you think you are, you can find a path that works for you. Just remember: go at your own pace—there is no rush!

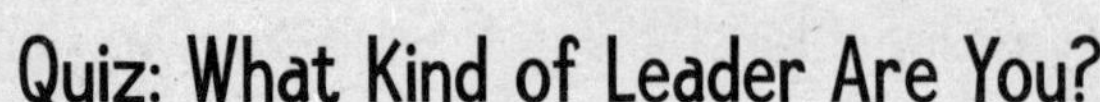

Quiz: What Kind of Leader Are You?

Leaders come in all shapes, sizes, and ways of being, and there is no one right or wrong way to lead. You just have to figure out what works for you, your team, and your project, and you can go from there. Discover what type of leader you are by taking this quiz!

1. You're hosting a slumber party, and the pizzas you ordered are an hour late. You're starving! What do you do?
   A. Call the pizza place and tell them they're so late they need to throw in free breadsticks. Also, can you have a discount?
   B. Go into the kitchen, chop some veggies, and arrange a veggie platter for your friends.
   C. Ask everyone what movie they'd like to watch. A movie will distract everyone from their rumbling stomachs!

2. Your entire grade is selling chocolate bars to help pay for an overnight field trip. You and your friends have decided you'll be a lot more effective (and have more fun) if you sell your chocolate bars as a group. You decide to:.
   A. Call your local grocery store and see if it's okay to set up a booth outside it from 11:00 to 1:00 this Sunday. Then email all your friends and assign them different jobs at the booth.
   B. Get out your markers and some posterboard and start to make signs.
   C. Make a pledge to be there (wherever "there" is) as much as your friends need you, then show up right on time and stay the full two hours.

3. You break your arm and can't play in the big basketball game you've been excited about for weeks. You decide to:.

A. Ask your coach if you can be her assistant coach during practices and the game.

B. Paint your cast team colors.

C. Sit in the front row and cheer as loud as you can during the game.

4. There's a girl in your class whose mom was in a car accident, and she's worried they're going to have trouble paying bills because her mom won't be able to work for a few weeks..

A. Set up a crowdfunding campaign and email your friends, family, and classmates about contributing to it.

B. Bake a few casseroles and some cookies for them, then approach your classmates with the idea of creating a Meal Train. One class member would deliver dinner to your classmate and her mom every night.

C. Call her every day and visit her as much as you can. You know she's scared and lonely.

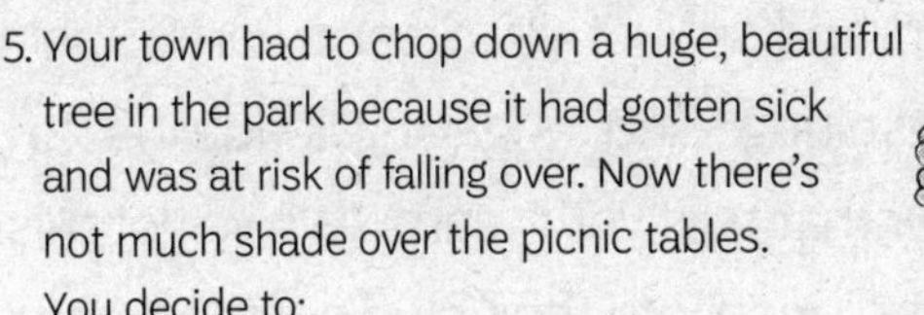

5. Your town had to chop down a huge, beautiful tree in the park because it had gotten sick and was at risk of falling over. Now there's not much shade over the picnic tables. You decide to:

A. Assemble and organize a group that will petition the town council to plant a new tree as soon as possible.

B. Why do the picnic tables need to be in that particular spot? Get your friends together and move the picnic tables under another tree.

C. Join the group that's petitioning the town council *and* help move the picnic tables!

Answers:

Mostly A: You are Organized and in Charge. You like to come up with a straightforward plan, execute it, and build a team to make things happen. Your leadership style is amazing and effective, but be careful about doing too much or trying to take control of everything! Your team will be excited and empowered when you give them the opportunity to contribute in meaningful ways.

Mostly B: You are Creative with Big Ideas. You think outside the box, love to engage people in a visual way, and inspire others to make service fun. Be careful to always have a plan, though! Creativity can be organized and engaging.

Mostly C: You are a Listener and Team Player. You trust the team you're on and are dedicated to helping wherever you're needed. Be sure your voice isn't lost and remember that just because you're supportive of everyone, you do not need to do all the work!

Your Mission Statement

No matter what kind of leader you identified yourself as being—or that you dream of being—remember that you are the heart and soul of your team. Part of being a motivating, inspiring, and engaging leader is to a radiate an energy that tells your team, "We've got this!" Your team wants to lean into their own personal power *and* the excitement of the team effort.

Your vision can spark that excitement. One of the easiest ways to present that vision is to create a mission statement. A mission statement is a pledge that you and your team will work as a unified front to take action. It highlights your cause, presents goals and strategy for reaching those goals, outlines benchmarks for how you'll know when you've reached your goal, and says, "This is what we're going to do." This puts all kinds of powerful energy out front and rallies your team to make good things happen.

Mission statements are straightforward and usually only a few sentences long, but they should always be clear. Think more about the message and energy than the number of words. When you read your mission statement, do you feel excited, inspired, and powerful? Do you feel like you're part of a team that's going to check their biases, respect one another, and work together? That's a great mission statement!

Journaling: Create a Mission Statement

Here's a mission statement to get you thinking. What are your ideas for a mission statement? Write them down in your journal.

The leaders of HELP THE STRAY CATS pledge to care for our neighborhood's stray cat population and help them find forever homes. We will do so by:

- Raising funds to spay and neuter the stray cats.
- Work with a local group to rescue the stray cats and kittens who can be domesticated.
- Raising awareness about how to feed and care for any cats who can't be rescued.

Goal: We have identified 10 stray cats. Within three months, we hope to rehome, spay or neuter, or provide shelter for 7 of them.

As members of a multicultural community of various ages and backgrounds, we promise to listen to each other's ideas, support our common goals, and respect one another. We will celebrate our differences and learn from each other every day as we create a sustainable solution.

Your First Meeting

Now that you have your mission statement, it's time to call your team together. Here's where the fun really begins! You're ready to take action!

Your first meeting is a great opportunity for everyone to get to know each other. If the meeting is in person, bring name tags. If it's online, try to make sure everyone has their camera on. You can play a team building game like those in Chapter 4, or simply go around the room and have everyone do this:

- Say their name.
- Say what they bring to your project (for example, they volunteer at a shelter or they raised a ton of money at their school fundraiser last year and are great at getting community donations).
- Answer a question that you've asked the group, like their favorite movie or where they'd travel if they could go anywhere in the world.

At your first meeting, you can also focus on what

everyone thinks the group should do to become a great team, like "listen to others without interrupting" or "bring three new ideas to each meeting." When team members give their input, they feel included and valued. Write these suggestions on a large piece of paper and post it on the wall (along with your mission statement) whenever you have team meetings.

Narrow Your Focus

At future meetings, you'll be ready to move on from the "get to know you" phase of planning. Before you are ready to start making a plan to accomplish your solution, you need to see whether it is realistic.

First, look at your mission statement. Does it outline your goal or goals? Check? Check! Does your mission statement set at least one benchmark and explain how you'll know when you've reached it? Check? Check! (Again, you may have many smaller steps along the way to reaching your ultimate goal.) Now, go around the room (or online meeting) and see how your team members feel about your goal or goals. Are there too many? Are they doable? You don't have to decide at that moment. For now, simply listen to your team's thoughts and evaluate their feedback later.

For example, if your group is trying to help the

stray cats in your neighborhood, the veterinarian on your team might say that your goal of trying to catch and spay or neuter *all* of them is unrealistic. You might be disappointed to hear this, but she is an expert! Think about what she said and make a note to yourself that maybe you should update your goal to spaying or neutering some of them. Then follow up with the vet later.

As you think about and refine your goal, it's also time to revisit the resources you have available to you. If you haven't created a resource list, go back to Chapter 3 and do it now. Take a look at this list and ask yourself: Do I have what I need? Do I know how to get it? Can my team help me? If you don't have the time, the money, and the adult involvement (or more) that you need to take action, it's okay. You can always narrow your focus! Sometimes not having the right resources is the main reason why goals change. And on the flip side, sometimes you'll discover you have so much money, time, or other valuable resources that you can widen your focus!

Just remember that narrowing down your goals and solutions is perfectly normal in the planning stages of a project. You can only do your best and tackle your issue a bit at a time. A sustainable solution *isn't* one that burns you out or can't be maintained in the long term. A sustainable solution may also start small, then grow over time as people learn about it and your amazing efforts!

She's Got This!

Hannah M. was only four years old, and she couldn't go to the park like other kids her age because she'd had a heart transplant that weakened her immune system. When a group of local girls saw her story on social media, they thought she might want an amazing place to play in her own backyard. The girls approached Hannah's mom, and she said this sounded like a terrific idea.

First, the girls researched safe playground equipment for people with weak immune systems, and discovered what was and wasn't safe for her. The girls consulted with experts on their ideas. Then they made a plan and set a goal.

They created a list of necessary supplies and assessed their existing resources. They weren't

able to construct something completely by themselves, so they asked one of their dads, who worked in construction, to help. They came up with a budget. When they realized they needed to raise funds they held a bake sale, sold some of their toys, and did extra chores for allowance. Soon they had $900 to spend!

With a few other handy adults, they built a backyard playhouse for Hannah M. and stocked it with toys so she could play outside anytime she wanted.

Create Steps

Hannah M.'s backyard playhouse came together because of focus, good planning, talking with experts, the use of available resources, and teamwork. It took time, but the girls put steps in place that helped them reach their benchmarks and make their goal a reality. If they did it, so can you!

Creating easy-to-follow, actionable steps will help you take action and make your project run smoothly, so talk to your team about their ideas, goals, and plans. These steps may include:

Collect resources: What materials do you we have? What donations do we need to ask for? What will we need to buy? When will we ask for donations and/or go shopping? What experts and volunteers can help?

Fundraise: Are you going to need more money? When and how will you raise the money?

Site visits: Are you going to need to visit the area where you're taking action? For example, the girls who wanted to help Hannah M. had to make a few trips to her backyard, first to scope it out, then to take measurements, then to deliver supplies and build. If you need to travel, how do you plan on getting there and back?

Getting the word out: Will you need to engage the support of your community? Do you have to post flyers? Would attending a town council or other community meeting help you?

Permits/legal matters: Yes, you might need to talk to officials about getting permits or permission to do certain things to raise money, spread awareness, or host events in your community. You might require a food handler permit if you want to host a spaghetti dinner fundraiser, for example, or if you're holding a rally in a public place, you will definitely need permission from your town. Getting permissions or paperwork from officials takes time, so build a couple extra weeks (or even months) into your schedule for them.

Dividing Up Tasks and Responsibilities

Every member on your team is going to bring a special set of skills and interests to your project, and so is every volunteer. But it's your job as leader to create a list of tasks, responsibilities, and timelines, then assign team members to each job. Or you can ask your team to sign up for what *they* want to do—just make sure they don't all sign up for the same thing! Make sure no one is overwhelmed with too many tasks because you don't want anyone to burn out. That goes for you, too! While it might be tempting to do all the work by yourself, when you're stepping up to make the world a better place, it's helpful and more fun to share responsibilities with volunteers and members of your team.

Try these steps to divide up tasks and responsibilities and keep your project on track:

Think about strengths: Remember the list of strengths that your team members created at your first meeting? When you're considering who can tackle which task, take a look at it. If a member of your team is great at drawing, maybe they should design flyers. If someone else is a natural at public speaking, perhaps you should ask if they want to speak at the next town meeting, where you're advocating for your cause. Team members and volunteers love to feel noticed and respected, so when you point out what your teammates are good at, they may feel happy that you are valuing their strengths.

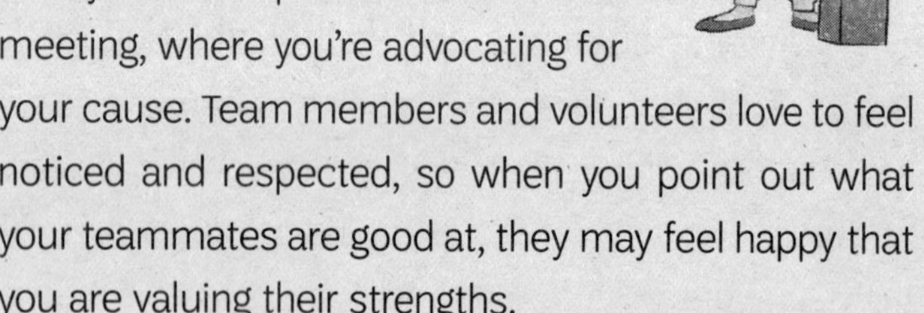

Consider committees: If you divide your project into categories of its big needs, you can then have different members of your team head up those committees. For example, if you're working to help the stray cats in your neighborhood, the vet on your team could oversee the spay/neuter committee, and your friend who loves social media could be in charge of the influencer committee. As the leader, you could oversee them and all the other committees working on your project. Remember also: You're a team, and people on teams work together so nobody has to do anything alone. Committees can also really help with burnout because they make it easier for people to focus on their specific jobs.

Set timelines: Timelines aren't deadlines, but it can be helpful to settle on a date (or a rough date, it doesn't need to be exact) when each part of the project needs to be finished. Because being on a team means working *together,* emphasize that it's important to try to stick to these dates as much as possible. But if things come up, don't stress or get angry. You're all volunteers, after all. Even *you* are a volunteer!

Check on progress: At each team meeting, check in to see the progress that's being made. As a team, talk about your tasks. What's working and what's not working? You might have to be flexible and switch assignments around or add more tasks—or take some away. Try not to look at jobs that fall to the wayside or are hard to accomplish as signs of failure. Success is learning to adapt and change plans when you need to, and good teamwork allows that to happen.

Stay organized: Staying organized is vital to keeping a project moving along. Keeping track of what tasks you have done and need to do and what tasks you've put others in charge of will help. Need help staying organized? This could be one of the tasks you give to a team member! If you choose to work online, there are also some terrific platforms that can make organization and communication easy. You can create committees online, communicate with those committees all in one place, and stay on top of everything without a million emails flying around. Work with an adult to help you set up a Slack channel, Google classroom, or another online platform that can support you and your team.

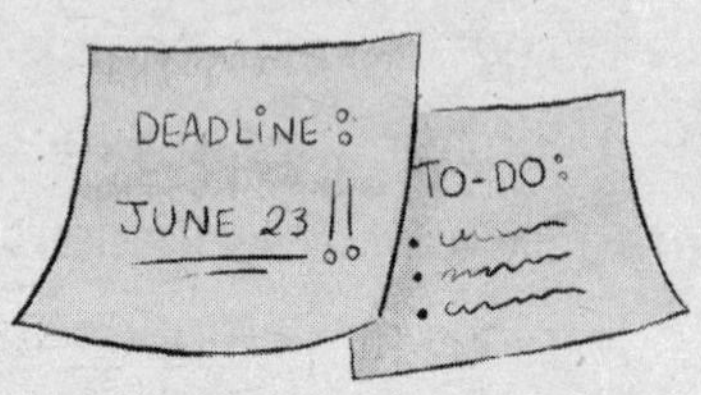

Keep notes: Finally, keep good notes about what you're doing, and take photos or videos about your projects so you can share them with the community or pass them to future volunteers. Photos, videos of important moments, and even notes from your meetings will help you and your team see how far you've come and keep everyone motivated and excited about the project.

Journaling: Create a Planning Table

Here is a sample planning table the "Help the Stray Cats" team might use. You can follow it or adapt it based on your team's needs and vision.

What Is the Task?	How Will the Task Be Done?	When Will the Task Be Done?	Which Team Member(s) Should Complete the Task?
Gather information about number of cats in the neighborhood.	Go door to door with an adult to ask identifying details about cats. Make a list of cats.	November 25	Sarah Anne Antonia Naiyhah
Talk to an expert to find out what cats need. (Do they want to live outside? Do they prefer homes?)	Visit Dr. Johnson at the local vet clinic—she's a friend of Sarah's mom.	November 30	Sarah
Research best habitats for outdoor cats.	Research on the internet. Talk to Dr. Johnson. Ask a pet shelter.	November 30	Rachel Anne
Find out how a pet shelter can help.	Ask the pet shelter if they take stray cats.	December 15	Naiyhah Antonia
Find out cost of spaying or neutering a cat.	See if Dr. Johnson (if she can help!) can speak to her staff to see how much they spend on spaying/neutering and if they can do it at a lower rate.	December 15	Dr. Johnson
Raise community awareness about what we're doing.	Take photos of cats and put them on flyers. Come up with wording for the flyers. Print flyers out and put them in people's mailboxes. Put flyers on NextDoor.	January 15	Janelle Frida Sally

Build Your Budget

Some projects are expensive, and others don't cost much, especially if you've gotten local businesses to donate items you need. Regardless, you probably will need *some* money to buy supplies, print flyers, apply for permits, and more. Depending on your monetary needs and available resources, you may either need to raise more money or narrow your focus. Or—if you've been planning way ahead—you might have tons of money because you had a super-successful lemonade stand last month or have been babysitting every weekend for the last year. In that case, you may not have to *worry* about money, but you will need to think about it no matter what.

Making a budget is an essential step when you take action. A good budget will show you how and where you spend your money, as well as when you should save it. Just know that a budget isn't set in stone. As your needs grow, it may grow too. Just be sure to have ideas of how to raise *more* money.

A budget should always take into account these three things:

1. **Your values:** Do the things you want to spend your money on align with your values? If you use your money toward a certain task, object, or objective, does it line up with what you believe in and what your team wants? For example, if your team cares deeply about the environment, consider purchasing used goods and supplies or buying new items you can donate, sell, or use multiple times. Do the places you're buying supplies from support your values? For example, you could buy the items you need online for a little cheaper than another place in town, but you've heard the company discriminates against certain communities and treats their workers badly. Plus, all the packaging that comes with shipping is bad for the environment. Would you rather shop locally to support your local community (and avoid supporting a company that doesn't represent your values) or is the convenience of ordering online and saving a little money more important?

2. **Your priorities:** Before you spend any money or budget for something, ask yourself: Is this a smart way to spend money? Do you really *need* this, and is it going to add to your goal, steps, or solution in a meaningful way? Or can you, your team, and your project do without it?

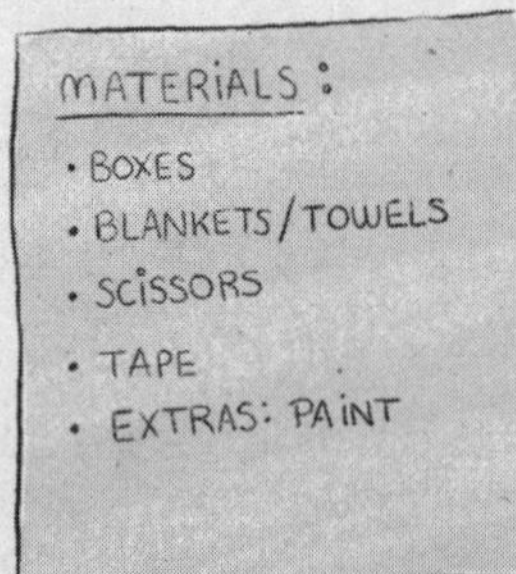

3. **Can I afford it?** If something is way too expensive for your group to afford, you'll need to evaluate your priorities and values. Maybe you can technically afford something, but it would mean that you'd have no money left for other important needs. Is there a less expensive alternative? Can you ask for a discount? Might a community member or business be interested in donating this?

Journaling: Build Your Budget

Make a table like this to create your budget. Go back to your list of resources and needs and copy the items into the What You Need column of this chart. Use a pencil in case you need to take some items away or add a few as your project moves forward. Or you can create a spreadsheet on the computer. Ask an adult to help if you feel stuck!

What You Need	Ask for a Donation From . . .	Donated? Yes/No	Cost of Items to Get That Haven't Been Donated
Example: Paper for signs to post around the neighborhood, tape and markers to create signs	Sarah's dad's office	Yes	$0
Example: Healthy food to feed stray cats	the local pet food store	No	$50
Example: Boxes for temporary cat habitat	the bookstore—they always have boxes!	Yes	$0
Example: Towels and blankets for temporary cat habitat	my parents to donate what we have at home	Yes	$20
		TOTAL AMOUNT TO FUNDRAISE:	$70

As you can see, a budget lets you know how much money you need to raise. There are many ways to come up with that money: you can ask for donations, work to earn it (babysitting, doing chores for family or neighbors, pet sitting, and more), or sell items like baked goods, bracelets, or old toys. You may even have money in savings you want to contribute.

After you pool your money, evaluate if you have enough to meet your budget's needs. If you don't, either narrow your focus or raise more. If you have extra money after you build your budget, price out your supplies and shop for what you need, lucky you! You can save the money to use later, treat the team to an ice cream party (don't forget the whipped cream!), or donate the money to a cause related to your project. If you discover that you need *more cash*, you'll need to narrow the focus of your project, eliminate some supplies, raise funds, or ask for donations.

Not sure how to ask for donations? Try starting with a letter like this:

Dear Hardware Store Manager:

My name is Veronica G., and I am a fifth grader at PS 289 in Centerville, South Carolina. I recently noticed that the outdoor area around Centerville Central Library is full of weeds, and the flowers, bushes, and plants that used to make the garden look so beautiful are all gone or dead.

I talked with the librarian and learned that our city didn't include the funds to plant a garden around the library in this year's budget. I have decided, along with my fellow fifth graders, a team of librarians who want to help, and a few of our caregivers, to create a garden club at the library. Our goal is to weed the garden and plant new flowers and plants so everyone will have a beautiful garden to enjoy. We would like the Garden Club to meet once a month to plan garden maintenance, purchase books about gardening for the library, and host events for the community so everyone can learn how to care for their gardens.

To make this all happen, we've created a budget but don't have all the funds we need yet, and we were wondering if you might be able to help us. Would you be able to donate some gardening supplies we know we'll need, including a few rakes, shovels, trowels, and spades? Anything you could provide, including planting soil, mulch, or flowers would be so appreciated by our whole community. If you cannot donate supplies, a cash donation would be put to good use in helping us get the things we need to make our garden a reality. And of course, if you can't donate, we are still so grateful for your time, and we hope to see you at the local library. Be on the lookout for the new garden-it's going to be great!

Your neighbor,
Veronica G.

If a community member or business makes a donation, make sure they know how grateful you are and let them know how their donation made a difference! Here's a sample thank-you letter:

Dear Hardware Store Manager:

Thank you so much for your very generous donation of three rakes, two trowels, two spades, and five bags of mulch, which helped our newly formed Centerville Central Library Garden Club plant a new garden! I hope you can stop by and see the beautiful bushes and flowers your gift helped us plant (if not, here is a photo!). Without you, we would not have been able to clean up the area, design a new garden, or add pretty new plants. We know that library visitors will enjoy it for years to come, and for that, we thank you.

Your neighbor,
Veronica G.

Communicate with Your Team

Keeping clear, regular lines of communication with your team and volunteers is super important. People like to feel heard, respected, and needed! If someone reaches out to you or does something to help out, it's good to reply or let them know how much you appreciate them. Creating a personal connection with your volunteers is a great way to make them passionate about your cause. Other ways to communicate with your volunteers may be through a social media site, group texts, or regular meetings. Just remember that when people are kept in the loop about what you're doing, they're more likely to know you value them—which is important, because you do!

Create a Timeline

Making the world a better place takes time—plain and simple. There's no need to rush or put crazy pressure on yourself, but a timeline can help you in lots of ways.

Putting your project on a schedule helps you stay focused, see how you're making progress, and decide whether you need to add to your to-do list or delete tasks along the way. A timeline is the heartbeat behind making any plan come to life and a helpful way to keep track of all you've accomplished. Here are two easy ways to start one:

1. Write down your list of tasks. You may already

have these on your planning table (see Chapter Seven). If not, write them down now!

2. Estimate how much time each task will take, taking into consideration your other commitments and the schedules of those you need to meet with and work alongside. You might want to add some extra time in, just in case unexpected challenges come up. Then, look at a calendar and count that number of days forward from the expected start date on your calendar. Record the start and end dates on your timeline.

After you've laid out each task and its deadline, you'll see how long your project will probably take. Keep your timeline on the wall or close to the area you use for meetings and planning, and use a sticker or marker to show the point you're at today so you can easily track how much you've done, how far you've come, and look forward to what's next. If you fall behind where you want to be or realize some parts of your project will take more time than you thought, no big deal! Just adjust your timeline and go from there.

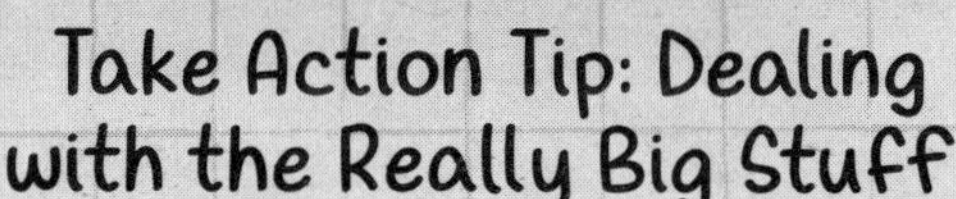

Take Action Tip: Dealing with the Really Big Stuff

Everyone knows there are big issues in the world right now, from climate change and poverty to years-long wars. Trying to fix global issues you care about may feel really difficult, if not impossible. Don't let that get you down. While you have a voice, a huge heart, and incredible abilities, you are not responsible for righting the wrongs of governments and big corporations—and those are the groups who make most of the decisions that cause issues in the world!

But don't give up. There are many people across the world and throughout history who have banded together with friends, classmates, and even total strangers to fight for global change. You are just one person, but one person plus their friends, plus those people's friends, adds up quickly and your team can grow faster than you'd think. (Think about it: if you have ten friends that ask ten more friends for help, and each of them ask ten more friends, you're up to a thousand people to help your cause!) Once you've got a lot of people involved, you become a huge, influential group with wide-reaching power. Together, you've got this!

Finally, if you set goals and reach them, you are also making an amazing difference toward a big global solution. Even small goals add up to big contributions!

CHAPTER EIGHT: MAKE IT HAPPEN

You've got your dream team, some solid goals, a few doable steps, lots of resources including helpful adults, enough money, and a timeline that gives you plenty of wiggle room. You're doing great stuff here!

Now, take a deep breath. You have already come so far from the first moment you decided you want to make a positive change in the world. In just a short time, you have done *so* much just by expressing the desire to help and reminding others that they have the power to make a difference in the world, too. Whatever lies ahead as you put your plan into action, remember to have fun, make time for yourself, and to celebrate the small wins along the way.

Lights, camera . . . take action!

Overcoming Obstacles, Setbacks, and Blind Spots

It's time for an emotional check-in! How are you feeling? Are you overwhelmed, or are you excited? Are you full of ideas, or do you think you've hit a (temporary) dead end? No matter where your head is, know that there is no wrong or right emotion when you take on a Take Action project. You may be happy one minute and so annoyed the next. A big reason for that is—no matter how much you prepare—you will probably encounter some obstacles and setbacks when you set out to make the world a better place.

One of those setbacks may involve other people. In fact, when you're working to make a difference in the world, you may face rude words and actions from people who don't share your views, and that may make you think twice about what you're doing. Don't let them steer you off course. Though you may feel all kinds of tough emotions, you can still count yourself among the bravest people in history. Even under the most difficult circumstances or facing the toughest odds, you can still take action.

Brave, talented, and diverse kids (just like you) have

faced discrimination, racism, sexism, homophobia, fear, self-doubt, and more as they worked to make the world a better place. They fought battles and withstood obstacles they never saw coming. But guess what? They kept going. And so can you. If you've followed the steps and examples of this book and have a fierce attitude inside you, you *are* going to take action and make real change.

She's Got This!

Jordan R. was born without the bottom half of her arm, and throughout her life she's had plenty of people give her strange looks and ask her "what happened to you?" or assume that she can't do as much as everyone else because she's differently abled. Instead of letting that discrimination make her feel bad about herself, Jordan became determined. She decided to use what makes her different to create positive change in the world.

When she was thirteen, Jordan realized she didn't like the fact that artificial limbs—called prosthetics—are often viewed as unusual or awkward. She started working with a designer and came up with a plan to create a prosthetic arm that shoots out glitter. The purple, glitter-shooting arm they eventually created caught the attention of numerous television programs—and Mark Cuban from *Shark Tank!* Jordan and her mom were so inspired by the joy the prosthetic arm brought to others that she started two nonprofits for disabled youth: one to help empower them through STEM activities and the other to teach them innovative design skills.

"It's so cool to just be able to talk to other people with disabilities, someone who's like you—that's so important in life," says Jordan. "It makes you feel less alone. Working together to build off our differences and make some really interesting, useful stuff—it's just awesome. It reminds you that being different is actually a huge opportunity."

Growing up, people's stares had made Jordan angry. But she used her feelings of anger and frustration to create change and build bridges. Her efforts have led to increased representation for people with disabilities, including in American Girl and Barbie products. Think about what makes you upset or angry, and how you might tap into those feelings to find new ways of making the world a better place.

Another obstacle you may face is exhaustion or feeling like you're not getting anywhere. Maybe you were exhausted from a hard week at school, yet you still had to get up at seven a.m. on Saturday to speak to a pet shelter director about cat care. Or possibly it rained unexpectedly the day you posted flyers around your neighborhood—and you didn't have an umbrella. Feel like you're on an emotional rollercoaster? That's normal. You don't have to love every part of your Take Action journey. Some days might feel lousy, and that's okay! What matters is that you are *taking action.* You are helping to change the world because you joined with others to become a part of a solution.

The key is to *learn* from the things that make you stop in your tracks. If you encounter a setback or face an obstacle, take a minute to breathe, then try to use it as an opportunity.

Obstacles can help you stretch a little farther, try a little harder, or practice a part of your personality you haven't been using. For example, if someone on your team is being unkind and unhelpful, you can view that as an opportunity for you to practice patience and communication. Or pretend you've devised a plan to construct shelves on your block for a "free store" where people can donate winter clothes. You see the need for this because there's no secondhand store within miles of your urban neighborhood, and you know, with winter coming up, many people need coats. Suddenly, the spot where you planned to construct your shelves becomes a construction zone, so you have to find somewhere else. Don't give up! You can use this as an opportunity to explore other parts of your neighborhood. Maybe you'll even meet new people!

When (not if!) you encounter setbacks or face obstacles, just remember:

- **You can always adjust your plan or make a new plan.**
- **You are not alone. You have a team, and you can ask them for help.**
- **It's okay to feel sad or frustrated. Everyone deals with setbacks, and while this feeling is temporary, it's still hard. Feel your feelings!**
- **Believe it or not, obstacles can make you tougher, more creative, and better at bouncing back from**

other obstacles in your future. The difficult stuff doesn't feel great, but it does help you grow.

Through your project—and in life!—you will also face blind spots. Blind spots are issues or challenges you didn't see coming but were right there all along. For example, if you are trying to help stray cats, you might encounter a blind spot when you discover that one cat just *won't* eat your food or be captured. That cat has been his own independent creature the whole time, but you didn't see it—or chose not to see it. You were hoping you'd help *all* the cats, but some of them might not actually want the help you're offering, and that's okay. You can make the best plans in the world, but there will still be unexpected setbacks. You can't anticipate these things, only deal with them. We all make mistakes or fall short of where we want to be. What do you do when that happens? You learn something and grow stronger.

Journaling: Setback Table

When you encounter an issue, setback, obstacle, or blind spot, it's helpful to take a second to think about how far you've come and what you've learned. Remember that obstacles are opportunities, so write down what you can learn from them. You can create a page in your journal like this for setbacks you experience to help you get through them, learn from them, and move on.

What happened:

What I learned:

What I can do about it:

When the Team Isn't Getting Along

Everyone on your team is going to be a little bit different, and honestly that's amazing. Life would be so boring if we all looked, acted, and felt the same. Differences can also be challenging, though. People won't always get along or agree on every aspect of your plan. As your team's leader, you are responsible for navigating the highs and the lows of working with other people. Some days everything will be amazing, and other days will be chaos. There are so many ways to deal with different personalities and conflicts between people, but these are the things you should try to remember:

Listen: If you're having a conflict with someone on your team, or if two people aren't getting along, speak to them individually and listen closely to their concerns. To make sure you really get what they're saying or asking, repeat back to them what they've said to you, then have them tell you if you are understanding the issue properly.

Focus on the solution: Your job is to help your *cause* more than your *team,* but you need your team to make it all happen. As you try to work out issues or interpersonal conflict, work to bring everyone back around to the reason you're all there in the first place: the cause. Ask your team members to remember this, too. Point them to your mission statement and ask them to read it again. They might suddenly realize it's worth compromising on something they had wanted to do in order to make a difference in a bigger way.

Don't blame: Resist the urge to start blaming anyone, especially if there is conflict between two people. First, listen closely to both sides, and try to find common ground or a good compromise between the two people (maybe they can both work on the project, but they shouldn't work directly together!). But if it seems that someone isn't a good fit for the team, politely talk to them about stepping down. Just remember, this is an absolute last resort.

Nothing will ever go perfectly on a team, so remember that conflicts and differences of opinion are totally normal. Being a leader is a big job, and it might even feel overwhelming at times to be in charge. But you have the compassion, kindness, and vision to make it work.

Quiz: How Do You Keep the Peace?

Where there are personality issues or conflicts among team members, it's often up to the team leader to figure out a way to solve them. How would you do it? What does your peacekeeping style say about you as a leader?

1. There's a girl in your group who thinks she knows the answer to everything! Ther truth is that she knows a whole lot, but she is always talking more than everyone else and making her ideas heard first. It seems like no one else has an opportunity to contribute. You decide to:

   A. Let everyone have a chance to speak, but limit them to one minute each, and each answer must directly address the question you've posed.

   B. Break everyone into small groups. The groups rotate at each meeting with different leaders each time.

   C. Pull your friend aside and have a gentle talk about how she needs to give others space to share their ideas, too, for the good of the group. You love her ideas and want to keep them coming, but you need to make sure all voices are heard!

2. No one in your group can agree on a budget. Some people think you should spend *a lot*, which means you'd have to fundraise more than you expected and get donations. Other people think you can do it all on the cheap. Argh! How do you get everyone to agree?

   A. Ask everyone to share their ideas, then call for a vote on the best budget.

   B. Revisit your mission statement and emphasize that the *goal* matters more than how you get there. Break everyone into groups and ask them to talk through their differences until they can agree upon a solution. Give them ice cream and play your favorite music to make them happy and excited about being part of the team.

   C. Walk into your caregiver's workplace and ask the boss for a big donation. This will solve everyone's concerns because suddenly money won't be an issue. You've already got the letter all written up!

3. Everyone in your group has been so busy with school that they're falling behind on all their deadlines. No one is getting anything done on time, and you're worried the project is going to fall apart because of it. You:

A. Ask everyone to sit in a circle, talk about their feelings, and then ask everyone to recite your mission statement together.

B. Give your team a pep talk about self-care.

C. Adjust the timeline and present them to the group. You can figure this out!

4. Things are going so well with your project that you decide to make its reach bigger. When you tell the group, some of them are shocked that you want to add to their responsibilities. After the meeting they tell you they don't want to be a part of the group anymore. You decide to:

A. Take their feelings to heart and reassign their roles within your group.

B. Write them each personal notes that tell them how much you appreciate all their hard work. Then, ask them to give it a week before they make their decisions. All that week, email them notes of encouragement.

C. Immediately go out and recruit more people for your group.

5. Oh no! Someone went to the store to buy supplies, left the envelope full of cash they were using in the shopping cart, and then noticed the cash was missing! Everyone is upset at this person, and some people even want to kick them off the team. What do you do?

A. Tell the group that while what happened is a big setback, it was an honest mistake. Then you pull out your white board and ask everyone for their suggested solutions.

B. Group hug time! And then, you ask everyone to write one nice thing about each person in the group. You read the lists out loud, knowing this will create good feelings about each person—especially the team member who lost the money.

C. You visit the store and ask to speak with the manager. Did anyone turn in an envelope of cash they'd found? It's unlikely, but maybe someone saw it sitting in a cart and were worried someone else would steal it! If it doesn't turn up, you come up with a plan to raise more funds.

Answers:

Mostly A: Super Hear-O. As an empathetic leader, you truly listen to others and take their feelings to heart, then try to balance everyone's personalities for the good of the group. If you have a happy, well-balanced group, people are going to feel energized for your cause.

Mostly B: Cheer Captain. There's no doubt you're a motivational leader. When people disagree or have bad feelings, you rally to get them excited again. While you know not everyone will get along or be happy all the time, you have what it takes to inspire optimism and enthusiasm.

Mostly C: Executive Producer. There's no doubt, you're a problem solver to the core. When there are disagreements, issues, or conflicts, you find or create a solution. You always listen to your team's ideas, but you never come to the table without a strong plan of your own.

Self-Care and Burnout

Sometimes it just doesn't matter *what* the issue is or where it's coming from. If you're feeling stress, worry, anxiety, pain, or a million other unpleasant things that make your stomach do flips and your mind race, something's not right! Maybe you took on too much responsibility, tried to do too many things at once, created a plan that was just a little too big, or got into a huge fight with the person you thought was your number-one teammate. Ultimately, it doesn't matter how you got to Burnout Town, the point is, you're here, and you need a ticket to anywhere else, fast. Chances are, when you take a break and do something that makes the stress go away, you're going to be able to come back to your project and team with a clear head. Self-care is always a good idea.

There are so many ways to manage burnout and practice self-care when you're in the middle of taking action. Here are just a few ideas:

Talk to an adult or trusted mentor about how you're feeling: Tell them you don't need advice if you're just wanting to vent; you just need someone who can listen to you and provide comfort. Remember empathy?

That's what you need from them right now.

Get moving: It's scientifically proven to lower stress! Take a walk, get on your bike, dance, jump on the trampoline—whatever you like to do. Exercise produces something called endorphins, which are chemicals that circulate in your bloodstream and make you feel good. They're like your body's version of candy. Pretty sweet.

Turn to your favorite hobby: Don't forget about the other things that make you happy. Do you like to draw, dance, play video games, read, or make friendship bracelets? Do one of these things. A hobby is a terrific way to refocus and forget the things that are stressing you out.

Hugs: Hug your caregiver, hug your pet, hug your sibling, or hug your best friend. Feeling close to someone you love will lower your blood pressure and give you a moment's peace.

Hydrate and eat something: Sometimes when people are stressed out, they forget to drink enough water or stop to eat. Drink water throughout the day and at all meals, and eat a healthy breakfast, lunch, and dinner. Don't forget snacks!

Treat yourself: If you're feeling down, sometimes you need a quick way to feel up. Go to a movie, go see a friend, head to the dog park, or binge-watch your favorite TV show. It's okay to take a break and indulge yourself sometimes.

Do a different act of kindness: If you're so busy thinking about the details of your own project, sometimes it's nice to contribute to someone else's. Have you heard of karma? It's the idea that the energy you put out in the world will come back to you someday. Share your good energy by tutoring a younger kid, cleaning up your local park, or even just sticking a note in your neighbor's mailbox.

So Is it Working?

Your plan is moving along just fine! Or is it? With so many different people on your team doing so many different things all at once, how do you know when things are going smoothly—and when they aren't?

Time to huddle, team!

At every meeting—whether it's online or in person—you should ask for a status report related to everyone's tasks. Have people met their target deadlines? If they haven't, what do they still need to do? On the planning table you created (see Chapter 7), cross off dates or make notes about what still needs to be done. Add a column for follow-up notes to write down where everything stands. Your chart might look something like this:

What Is the Task?	How Will the Task Be Done?	When Will the Task Be Done?	Which Team Member(s) Should Complete the Task?	Follow-up Notes
Gather information about number of cats in the neighborhood.	Go door to door with an adult to ask identifying details about cats. Make a list of cats.	~~November 25~~ December 5	Sarah Anne Antonia Naiyhah	Need more time because of Thanksgiving! As of 11/15, 9 cats identified. We think there are 12 so still asking.
Talk to an expert to find out what cats need. (Do they want to live outside? Do they prefer homes?)	Visit Dr. Johnson at the local vet clinic—she's a friend of Sarah's mom.	November 30	Sarah	She is on board to help! Sarah has detailed notes about her conversation with Dr. Johnson.
Research best habitats for outdoor cats.	Research on the internet. Talk to Dr. Johnson. Ask a pet shelter.	~~November 30~~ December 15 (Anne to talk to hardware store)	Rachel Anne	Anne's dad will help us construct something! Anne to talk to hardware store about donating supplies.
Find out how a pet shelter can help.	Ask the pet shelter if they take stray cats.	~~December 15~~ January 15	Naiyhah Antonia	Pet shelter was very busy at the holidays. Ask again.
Find out cost of spaying or neutering a cat.	See if Dr. Johnson (if she can help!) can speak to her staff to see how much they spend on spaying/neutering and if they can do it at a lower rate.	December 15	Dr. Johnson	Yay! Dr. Johnson says the clinic can do this for free. FREE!
Raise community awareness about what we're doing.	Take photos of cats and put them on flyers. Come up with wording for the flyers. Print flyers out and put them in people's mailboxes. Put flyers on NextDoor.	January 15	Janelle Frida Courtney	9 photos taken Frida working on the flyer. Who has access to NextDoor?

Don't feel bad if something doesn't go according to your schedule! Think of your planning table as a living, breathing thing. You're going to watch it grow and change as you add to it and take items away from it regularly. There are no mistakes here; only different paths to finding the best solution.

Speaking of solutions, to see if your plan is taking you where you want to go, you need to look at whether it's heading toward your ultimate goal: a solution to an issue the world is facing!

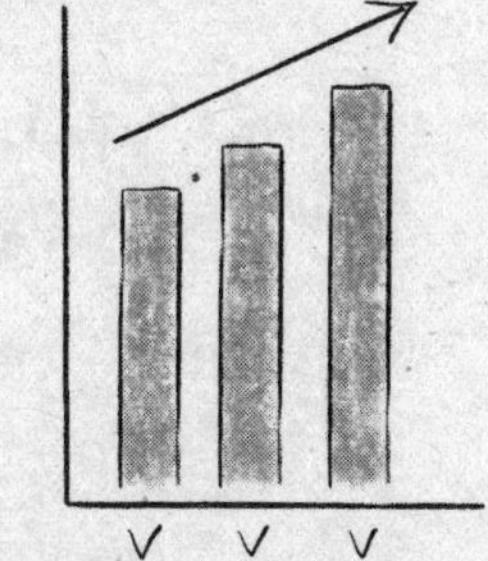

To see if you're meeting your goal, revisit your mission statement. Are you accomplishing the tasks you set forth? Are you close to your goal within your target dates? And have you worked as a team, honoring each other's strengths, differences, ideas, and personalities?

Remember as well that a good solution achieves one of the following:

- **Makes a change that is long lasting.**
- **Educates and inspires others to be part of the change.**
- **Changes a rule, regulation, or law.**

During each meeting, check in to see whether the tasks you're accomplishing meet one of these criteria. If they are, you're on the right track! If they're not, keep trying. Again, look at your mission statement. If you feel you're adhering to that, you're on course. If not, it's time to reevaluate your plan.

Take Action Tip: Create a Stressless Zone

Stress is part of any Take Action project, but there are ways to cope with it. One of them is to make a stressless comfort zone for yourself. This activity will allow you to find a place that will relax, soothe, and comfort you when things get to be a little too much.

Pick a peaceful spot in your home or outside that makes you feel happy. This place should be away from distractions like the television and family members who will try to talk to you.

Fill your space with things you love. For example, you might bring some boba tea, a warm blanket, your favorite stuffed animal, and your sketchbook and markers. No phones or electronic devices, please!

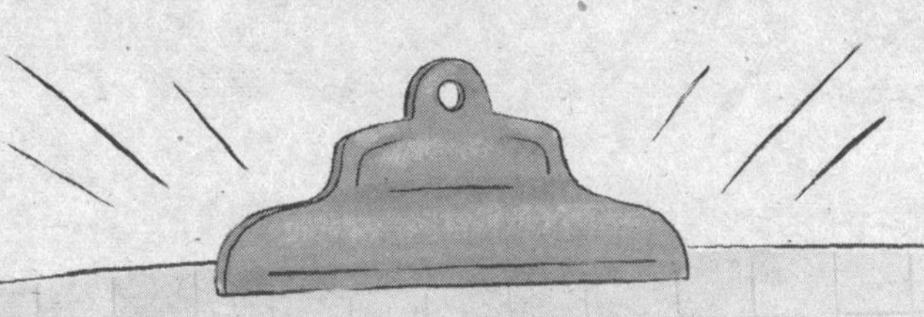

Set a timer for fifteen minutes and do an activity. It doesn't have to be a quiet activity! You can dance or sing—just so long as you're not stressing someone else out.

After fifteen minutes, stop your activity and reflect. Write down how you felt. Was the time challenging or enjoyable? Were you surprised by anything? If so, what?

CHAPTER NINE:

CELEBRATE—YOU DID IT!

You did it! You identified an issue you cared about, put together a team, figured out a practical and long-lasting solution, put your plan into action, and did *all kinds* of emotional work to make sure you were happy and settled when the process became stressful.

Sure, you may need to check in with your project and put out fires every now and then. For example, you might discover that a new stray cat has moved into the neighborhood and needs help. If you've educated and inspired other leaders to know how to help the cat, that's great! The new project leader may *still* have questions for you, though. But you've met your goals and created a sustainable solution. You're amazing. You took action, and you helped change the world!

CONGRATULATIONS! Now it's time to celebrate.

Sharing Your Story

After you've taken action and made positive change, you have every right to shout about it from the highest mountain in the world. Well, maybe not *exactly*. Mount Everest is really tall. But sharing your story in any way that brings your cause and its solutions into the spotlight is a great way to bring attention to the work you've done. People also *love* happy endings, especially if they involve young people like you doing amazing things. Have you rescued seven of the ten stray cats you wanted to help? Tell the world that!

Yes, it might feel awkward or overwhelming to shine a spotlight on yourself, but by bringing attention to your cause, you increase its impact. Sharing your story may bring in new volunteers, money, expert advice, and more. It also inspires others. They can learn from you, be motivated by your example, and get excited about taking action themselves.

Also, you're incredible! You deserve a ton of love for working so hard to make the world a better place.

Below are a few ways that you can share your story. Try to share as many of the steps from your plan as you can so people can really experience how you did it and get inspired to take on projects of their own. Show photos, lists, charts, meeting notes, or anything that reveals the many ways you got creative and made a difference. Seeing your efforts, your teamwork, and your amazing results is a way for people to know that taking action is collaborative, fun, and meaningful for you—and the people you're helping.

Ways to share your story include:

- Social media
- On a blog
- In your weekly email newsletter
- In an email
- Through a local newspaper or TV channel

- At your school
- At a presentation for a community group
- Through neighborhood signs

- On stickers that feature the name of your organization (be sure to indicate the address of your social media or website)

- **Ask your friends and family to share your story with their colleagues and friends**

Finally, when you share your story, don't forget to recognize and thank others. No matter how you took action, you had a team around you. That team included your family, friends, teachers, advisers, and community members, all of whom donated time and (maybe) money to your cause. Write thank-you notes to these people (by email or snail mail) and be sure to include the great news about your project's success.

Journaling: Write a Thank-You Letter

Here's a sample letter you could send to the people who've helped you along the way. In your journal, try to write a version of your own thank-you letter.

Dear Team:

Thank you for all your incredible help supporting our Help the Stray Cats initiative! I have been so fortunate to have the best family, mentors, friends, teachers, community members, and team supporting me in this cause I believe in so passionately.

I started this project on March 2, when I noticed a young mother cat and five kittens on the corner of Willoughby and Washington avenues. While many cats like being outside, outdoor cats–especially stray ones–are at a greater risk of illness, accidents, and early death. They also just don't get the love that so many house cats get.

After I spoke with my neighbors, I estimated that there were approximately ten stray cats in the five blocks around the intersection of Willoughby and Washington avenues. I decided that these cats need a solution! Those that can be captured should be spayed and neutered, and any that might thrive in homes should be given forever homes. If a cat just didn't want to move inside, I would construct a habitat for them to keep them warm and well-fed.

Our project has been a great success! So far, we've:

Identified ten stray cats.

Spayed and neutered seven of them with Dr. Johnson's vet clinic.

Gave six of them to shelters who are in the process of finding forever homes.

Built a "Cat Castle" in one of our neighbor's backyards for the four remaining stray cats. He feeds them daily, and we are still attempting to catch them.

Here are some photos of our beloved cats! The Help the Stray Cats initiative is still going, and we will continue to identify any new cats in the neighborhood and then help them.

We couldn't have done any of this without you! Thank you for your support, encouragement, love, and passion. From the bottom of my heart, I am grateful for all you've done.

Sincerely,
Emma R.

Party Time!

Now is the time to take some time for *you*. Refer back to the self-care list in Chapter 6 and do any of these things to reward yourself. Or go bigger! Throw a party,

go to an amusement park, enjoy a day at the beach, or head with your besties to your favorite ice cream shop (because *you deserve it*).

As you reward yourself, reflect on all you've accomplished. You have done a fantastic job, and you should feel awesome about that. Make sure you stop and take time to be thankful for yourself and your team. Gratitude is a great way to reinforce good feelings and positive events in your life, so spend some moments thinking about all that you're thankful for.

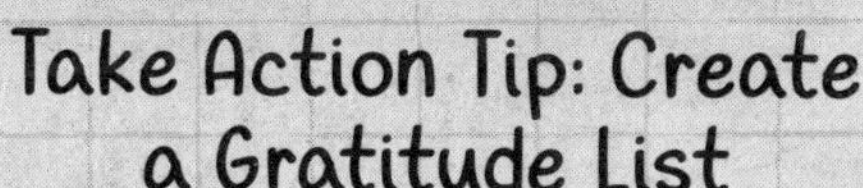

Take Action Tip: Create a Gratitude List

Create a list of all that you're grateful for from the beginning through the end of your Take Action project. You can read and reflect on this list next week, next year, or when you're seventy-five years old! It will keep you going and motivated to make the world a better place, especially in the moments when it's challenging. A sample list of what you're thankful for might include:

I am grateful for Joy—she brought cupcakes for our third meeting. I have the best friends!

I am grateful I learned how to create a budget because I'll use that skill the rest of my life.

I am grateful for my family, who helped me make posters and hang them around the neighborhood.

CONCLUSION: DON'T STOP NOW

You did it! When you challenged yourself, stepped into your power, and took action, you chose to learn more about yourself, become a global citizen, and make a positive change in the world. Every action—big or small—that you make for the rest of your life will be shaped by all you learned through your project.

If you start a new project, this amazing knowledge will stay with you. Don't be afraid to revisit any past mistakes, challenges, or triumphs and take what you learned from them on your new path. You may even find that some of the team members who helped you in your first Take Action project may want to help you again. Why wouldn't they?! You are full of such good energy, and that inspires everyone!

Keep that good energy strong as you go out in the world and tackle new challenges. You got this!